Twayne's United States Authors Series

EDITOR OF THIS VOLUME

Lewis Leary

University of North Carolina, Chapel Hill

Horace Greeley

TUSAS 413

Horace Greeley

HORACE GREELEY

By ERIK S. LUNDE
Michigan State University

TWAYNE PUBLISHERS
A DIVISION OF G.K. HALL & CO., BOSTON

Library of Congress Cataloging in Publication Data

Lunde, Erik S. (Erik Sheldon)
Horace Greeley.

(Twayne's United States authors series ; TUSAS 413)
Bibliography: p. 131–34
Includes index.
1. Greeley, Horace, 1811–1872—Literary art.
I. Title. II. Series.
E415.9.G8L9   818'.209   81–1234
ISBN 0-8057-7343-6   AACR2

For Meg

Contents

About the Author

Erik Sheldon Lunde is Professor of American Thought and Language at Michigan State University in East Lansing, Michigan. A Harvard graduate, Lunde received the M.A. and Ph.D. degrees in American History from the University of Maryland. In his current department, Lunde teaches courses in writing, American film, and American studies. Lunde has also offered courses in the Department of History at the University in American Intellectual History and Recent American History. Among other institutions, Lunde has taught at Marquette University and the University of Michigan. He has published articles in American history and on American nationalism. With Truman Morrison, he is co-host of a local television series entitled "Conversation," a program appearing on WKAR-TV. Lunde resides in East Lansing with his wife Margaretta and their two children, Elizabeth and Robert.

Preface

Horace Greeley's life is itself worthy of serious study, and he has been the subject of several fine nineteenth- and twentieth-century biographies. These studies have covered his contributions as printer, editor, reformer, and politician. What concerns this treatment is not so much the life *per se*, but the majesty of thought and writing style of such a man.

This book has three main goals in regard to Greeley: to trace his major ideas as exhibited in his publications; to analyze his most important works in terms of lasting literary merit; and to examine his writing style. It does not attempt to give a definitive portrait of his life or to discuss all the major contributions of his many journalistic and political activities. Also, while there is a chapter on Greeley's editorials, this study does not attempt to present an exhaustive treatment of these. Several of the biographies have effectively drawn on Greeley's hundreds of editorials for part of their sources. Rather, the coverage of editorials is selective and suggestive. Instead, this work explores Greeley's more reflective works, his published books. Here is where more analysis and further examination are needed. Also, for emphasis, this study has concentrated most heavily on Greeley's views of the domestic scene.

There are many who through encouragement and support have made this study possible. Douglas Noverr of Michigan State University was the individual who first urged that I pursue this subject and who provided me with many ideas and insights about Horace Greeley. Also at Michigan State, Bernard Engel initially sponsored this work, and Blaine McKinley made several helpful revisions on portions of the manuscript; in addition, Robert Hudson, Floyd Barrows, Gordon Rohman, and David Anderson were helpful with their advice; Henry Silverman and the office staff of the Department of American Thought and Language gave support. Also, I am grateful to the university for providing me with several research grants to sustain research and to the able staff of the library at Michigan State University for endless service in providing me with materials and working space.

My mentor, George Callcott of the University of Maryland, first suggested some years ago that I work on spokespersons of American nationalism, and the late Adrienne Koch supplied me with many insights on the subject. Boyd Shafer of the University of Arizona and Frank Klement of Marquette University were most supportive. Credit should also go to Truman Morrison of Edgewood United Church.

I am grateful to members of the Chappaqua Historical Society, particularly Mrs. David Swertfager, Mrs. Clendon Lee, Mrs. Schmelke, and Mrs. Edward Wheeler, for providing me with materials and a pleasant day at Greeley's old homestead. I wish to thank Thomas Spira, editor of the *Canadian Review of Studies in Nationalism,* for permission to use portions of an article for this study; his assistant, Reginald Stuart, was most helpful with some revisions.

The staffs of the manuscript division of the Library of Congress, of the Historical Society of Pennsylvania, and of the New York Public Library also deserve thanks. Sylvia Bowman of Indiana University, former editor of the Twayne United States Authors Series, was most helpful as was Yvonne Preston, who assisted in the typing. I am grateful to Marty North, who did most of the typing and also to Jo Grandstaff. I wish to thank Lewis Leary, who critiqued this study for G. K. Hall, Christine E. Lamb, who served as assistant editor and Lucy D. Lovrien, production assistant. These members of my family merit special appreciation: my grandmother-in-law, the late Margaretta Hilles; my parents-in-law, Henry S. and Francis Lee Hilles; my parents, Anders S. and Eleanor Lunde; and lastly for endless patience and assistance, my wife, Margaretta, and my children, Elizabeth and Robert.

ERIK S. LUNDE

Michigan State University

Chronology

1811   Horace Greeley born, February 3, in Amherst, New Hampshire.

1821   January 1, family moves to Westhaven, Vermont.

1826   April 18, printer's apprenticeship, *Northern Spectator*, East Poultney, Vermont.

1831   February, employee, *Erie Gazette*, Erie, Pennsylvania. August 19, arrives New York City; November, employee, the *Evening Post*.

1832   Employee, *Spirit of the Times*.

1833   January 1, printer, the *Morning Post*.

1834   Editor with Jonas Winchester of the *New-Yorker;* March 22, first issue.

1836   July 5, marries Mary Y. Cheney of Connecticut.

1838   Editor, the *Jeffersonian*, sponsored by Thurlow Weed and William Seward; February 17, first issue; February 9, 1839, last issue.

1840   May 2, editor, the *Log Cabin;* May 2, first issue; supports strongly Whig presidential and vice-presidential candidates, William Henry Harrison and John Tyler.

1841   April 10, editor, the *New York Tribune;* July 31, business partnership with Thomas McElrath, *Tribune;* September 30, the *New-Yorker* and the *Log Cabin* merged into the *Weekly Tribune*.

1842   Suit for libel brought by James Fenimore Cooper.

1843   September 1, *Evening Tribune* begun.

1844   March, birth of Arthur Young Greeley ("Pickie"). Strongly supports Henry Clay for president.

1845   February 17, *Tribune* building burned; May 17, semiweekly *Tribune* begun.

1846   November 20 to May 20, 1847, views on Fourierism exchanged with Henry J. Raymond.

1847   Travels to check holdings on Lake Superior and to attend river and harbor convention, Chicago, Illinois. November, birth of Ida Greeley.

1848   November 7, elected to Congress for one session; serves from December to March.

1849   July 12, "Pickie" dies.

1850   January 19, elected first president of New York Typographical Union no. 6. July 16, close friend, Margaret Fuller, dies. *Hints Toward Reforms.*

1851   Visit to World's Fair, London Crystal Palace, and to the Continent. *Glances at Europe.*

1853   Purchase of seventy-five acres at Chappaqua, New York.

1854   Opposes Kansas-Nebraska bill. Ends partnership with Weed and Seward. Helps in formation of Republican party.

1855   Visits Europe; incarcerated briefly in Paris.

1856   January 24, caned by Congressman Albert Rust of Arkansas. Strongly supports Republican presidential candidate John Fremont. *A History of the Struggle for Slavery Extension or Restriction in the United States.*

1857   Birth of last child, Gabrielle Greeley.

1859   Travels to Far West in support of Transcontinental Railroad. *An Overland Journey.*

1860   Chosen as delegate to Republican national convention, Chicago; initially supports Edward Bates of Missouri, but switches allegiance to Abraham Lincoln of Illinois. Famous series of editorials on letting "erring sister" states secede.

1861   Strongly supports Union war effort.

1862   August 20, most famous editorial addressed to Abraham Lincoln, "Prayer of Twenty Millions," which urges immediate emancipation policy.

1863   January 1, hails final Emancipation Proclamation. July, *Tribune* building attacked in New York City riot.

1864   July 17–21, meets with Southern "peace commissioners," Niagara Falls, Canada; Lincoln allows the mission but recognizes its futility. After supporting "boomlet" for Salmon P. Chase, switches allegiance to Lincoln again. *The American Conflict,* volume 1.

1865   April, hails Union victory.

1866   *The American Conflict,* volume 2.

1867   One of signers of bail bond for Jefferson Davis.

1868   Reluctantly supports Ulysses Grant for President. *Recollections of a Busy Life.*

1869   *Essays Designed to Elucidate the Science of Political Economy.*

1871 *What I Know of Farming* and *Mr. Greeley's Letters from Texas*. Breaks with Grant to join Liberal Republican movement.

1872 May 3, nominated for presidency, Liberal Republican convention; B. Gratz Brown named running mate; Democrats confirm his nomination; resigns editorship of *Tribune;* September, goes on campaign tour. October 30, wife dies. November 5, defeated by Ulysses S. Grant. Editor again, *Tribune*. Greeley dies November 29; is buried in Greenwood Cemetery, Brooklyn.

CHAPTER 1

The Representative Man

IN HIS *Recollections*, written in the late 1860s, Horace Greeley remembered how many years earlier on July 4, 1826, he as a precocious lad of fifteen had witnessed a celebration of the fiftieth anniversary of American independence in East Poultney, Vermont, where he was employed as an apprentice printer. At that time, the impact of the American Revolution was still deeply felt.

As Greeley said, the "Revolutionary War was not yet thirty years bygone when I was born, and its passion, its prejudices, and its ballads were still current" throughout his native New England. At the festivities, several Revolutionary veterans were seated on the platform; to them the Revolution was alive: "In those times, we had always from twenty to fifty Revolutionary soldiers on the platform— veterans of seventy to ninety years, in whose eyes the recurrence of the nation's anniversary seemed to rekindle 'the light of other days.' " This celebration, Greeley said, brought forth large crowds. "The Declaration of Independence sounded far less antediluvian than it now does; the quarrel of the colonists with King George, if not recent, was yet real, and the old soldiers forgot for a day their rheumatism, their decrepitude, and their poverty, and were proud of their bygone perils and hardships and their abiding scars." Greeley stressed the Providential quality of the national destiny because of the remarkable and sad occurrence that both Thomas Jefferson, the Declaration's author, and John Adams, the Atlas of Independence, died on that very day. The union in death of the chief living representatives of the two mother colonies, Jefferson from Virginia in the South, and Adams from Massachusetts in the North, attested to the divine heritage of an absolute union, something which would remain central in all Greeley's political thought:

When we learned . . . that Thomas Jefferson and John Adams . . . had both died on that day, and that the messengers bearing South and North respectively, the tiding of their decease, had met in Philadelphia, under the shadow of that Hall in which our Independence was declared, it seemed that a Divine attestation had solemnly hallowed and sanctified the great anniversary by the impressive ministration of Death.

Greeley stated that while Americans still celebrated the Fourth, the earlier "glory has departed." Indeed, to Greeley, a rediscovery of private times past was also a recapturing of the nation's heritage.[1]

For many significant men and women of Greeley's generation were preoccupied with the quest for national identity, with the compelling necessity to discover a "usable past" and to justify a faith in the belief that Americans were one people, born in the Revolution and dedicated to the proposition that the American nation represented a unique mission for man in his search for freedom, individual power, and happiness. The volumes of George Bancroft, the pages of Transcendentalists like Ralph Waldo Emerson, the paintings of men like Thomas Cole and Asher B. Durand abounded with the optimistic faith in a fundamental culture, founded in a pastoral dream emphasizing the unlimited possibilities of the human condition. Despite the ugly sectional agonies of the 1840s and the breakdown of law and order of the 1850s, this belief in a basic national unity existed in every region, a belief in an American community which allowed for a rich diversity of individual belief and action and which stressed the expansive potential of human behavior rather than its limitations. As long as Americans assumed there was a common national spirit, a common national will, they worked toward articulating it. To many, there was a pervasive sense that Americans' basic cultural unity would keep the nation united. Greeley's life, as he retold it, stretched from the fiery idealism of the Revolution, with its great faith in a vital national future, to the greatest test of that idealism, the Civil War, after which many, unlike Greeley, would feel that the nation had lost its sense of mission.

I A Representative Man

Horace Greeley was in Ralph Waldo Emerson's phrase a truly representative man of the nineteenth century. During his lifetime, he was a major and creative sponsor of reform, in his support of Fourierist communities, peace movements, antislavery, labor, temperance, the high tariff; he had been a vegetarian, an apostle of manifest destiny, an antitobacconist, a teetotaler, an opponent of capital punishment. In his editorials during his leadership of the newspaper he founded, the *New York Tribune*, and in many other major works, he had a special impact on his audience, persuading many to adopt his farsighted attitudes.

Greeley was also significant because he had the distinction of being the only editor-journalist to be a presidential nominee of a major political party in the nineteenth century, and hence his life represented a drive for personal power which was carefully balanced with a concern for freedom. His thought was characterized by the unique tensions of his age, between pastoral yearnings and urban opportunities, between peace and war, between radical reform and political compromise, between transcendent idealism and materialism.

There has always been a continual need to explore his works to discover the intellectual consistencies and inconsistencies of his age. His writings on ante-bellum reform and the westward movement, on labor and on the Civil War are worth a fresh look. Furthermore, his orations in his presidential campaign, made especially poignant because of his wife's and his own death in the same year, revealed a developing sense of American nationalism in the aftermath of a tragic civil war. A close associate, Whitelaw Reid, described Greeley's campaign as "the most brilliant continuous exhibition of varied intellectual power ever made by a candidate in a presidential canvass."[2]

If there were any concept which Greeley consistently advocated, it was the principle of an American democratic culture. All his other ideas—on freedom, equality, American nationalism, individualism, expansion, education, minority right, experimentalism, socialism—blended into his commitment to democracy. An editorial which appeared in the *Tribune* while Greeley was visiting Europe in 1851 epitomized his commitment:

If democracy be what we believe, it must have a wider and more perfect application. It must create a new social as well as a new political system. It must reform the relations of labor, of property and of social life, nor stop till all servitude, all castes, all inequality of privilege have disappeared to give place to integral liberty, justice and fraternal cooperative relations.[3]

Greeley's life spanned one of the most significant eras in American history, a time which saw the transition of America from a nation of farmers to the origins of a modern industrial state, a period which historian Douglas Miller characterizes as the "birth of modern America." Of course, Greeley celebrated much of what was happening to his land, but he also had doubts about what historian Paul Nagel has called the nation's "sacred trust." Greeley's heritage stretched back to Puritan founders and forward to pioneers of the great West. Always an Easterner, he still celebrated Western development. A man who welcomed the new machinery, he also harkened back to agrarian roots. Having felt the radical optimism of the 1830s and

1840s, he was distressed by the deepening disillusionment of the divisive 1850s and the strain of Civil War. Yet he kept the faith, as he prodded the conscience of Americans through daily editorials of the highest quality, often much better than what modern columnists offer and certainly better than almost all contemporary editorials.

If he failed in his ultimate quest for power, he still achieved fame, amassed a good living, commanded respect. Because of his position as editor of the *Tribune*, there was rarely a major event on which he did not make a comment or take a stand. Basically, he emerged as the chief spokesperson of the conscience of many Americans. In his diatribes, he gave vent to the intricate discussions of Americans on major national issues. A reading of his editorials, written over a period of thirty-five years, invites the modern citizen to a penetrating glimpse of the minds of his forebears as they toiled with the crises of a momentous period. And if at times Greeley represented the worst of contemporary attitudes, he also exhibited the best. Analyzing Greeley's popularity gives one an optimistic sense of the gifts of the American heritage. Out of the darkness of the past, Greeley remains the voice of hope, of the creative spirit, of the party of light.

II *The Writer*

Because Greeley was such a significant figure, it is a pity that so much of his work is out of print and unavailable to much of the general public. Greeley left to posterity all forms of writing, and good writing it was: editorials, descriptive reports, autobiography, history, exposition, lectures, letters. His *Recollections*, long neglected, was one of the major autobiographies of the nineteenth century. And Greeley showed a capacity to shift his style with the requirements of the moment: hence as a reporter sending dispatches from the West, Europe, and Washington to the *Tribune*, he displayed a sharp, exciting flair. While many observers stated that Greeley's presence on the platform was disheveled and his voice marked with an annoying Yankee twang, his oral presentations, both lectures and campaign speeches, would read well more than a century later.

A man who had no formal education beyond his fourteenth year, Greeley could move comfortably from discussions of philosophy, religion, literature, political economy, agriculture to biting exposés of political and societal corruption to charming profiles of contemporaries. That there is much to dispute in Greeley's ideas and often exaggerated commentary, no one can deny; but beneath the apparent contradictions, hyperbole, and needless invectives, Greeley's ideas, examined closely, represented a consistent formulation. Certainly, poet John Greenleaf Whittier saw a consistency in Greeley. In a letter written shortly after Greeley's death, the poet said, "All that time I have known him as the educator of the people in liberty, temperance, integrity, and industry, uniformly taking the side of the poet, enslaved, or suffering of every color and nationality."[4]

Yet, in a puzzling fashion, Greeley, one of the most famous Americans of the nineteenth century, has fallen in reputation. Many individuals in today's younger generation have never heard of him. Most of his books are out of print, and one cannot usually read his major editorials without a microfilm reader. He has not been the subject of major biography for more than twenty years, and there are no anthologies of his best writing.

This gradual disappearance from American consciousness is partially understandable. The great newspaper he founded, the *New York Tribune*, the contribution for which he most wanted to be remembered, ended its domestic existence as the *Herald-Tribune* in 1966. For those nurtured in the radical perspective of the 1960s, his reform pronouncements seem rather tame and too moderate. While he consistently opposed slavery, he rejected the more exacting stand of Abolitionists and anti-Establishmentarians like William Lloyd Garrison. To those bred in the conservative skepticism of the 1950s, his invective and leftist posturing would seem disturbing. His experimental, flexible mind is difficult to assess, and he appears superficial to many.

The most famous saying for which he became known, "Go West, young man, go West" has much less meaning to a generation which has witnessed the population explosion on the West Coast and the bankruptcy of expansion in Southeast Asia. Also, historians have long since corrected the initial attribution of this quotation; as Greeley himself acknowledged, the originator of this statement was John Soule, an Indiana editor.

Yet Greeley was a public figure, considered deeply significant and powerful in his time. James Parton, in his charming book first published in 1855, stated that during the "last ten years or more, Horace Greeley has influenced a greater amount of thought and a greater number of characters, than any other individual who has lived in this land."[5] Exaggerated as this estimate was, it suggested the special impact Greeley had on his generation. Of course, Greeley's public involvement was reflected in his writing, but the question remains as to whether Greeley's vast collection of material, often composed hurriedly out of a busy life, has unique merit for readers of the late twentieth century. A study of his work has significance as a measure of popular attitudes of his time, but does he still speak to his country-men and those abroad many decades later? He hoped he would, and it is the contention here that he succeeded.

Greeley in thought and life-style represented a classless demo-cratic culture. In everything he did and said, he opposed aristocracy of all kinds. He was always approachable. Greeley the conservative was willing to preserve the best of the past, but he welcomed ex-perimentation. In describing his visit to the *Tribune* building, James Parton stated that it was

a very cheerful place. No one is oppressed or degraded. . . . The distinctions which there exist between one man and another are not artificial, but natural and necessary; foreman and editor, officeboy and head clerk, if they converse together at all, converse as friends and equals. . . . the republicanism of the Continent has come to a focus at the corner of Nassau and Spruce Streets. There it has its nearest approach to practical realization; thence proceeds its strongest expression.[6]

Greeley in being and thinking embodied the American dream. Much has been written about the generation of Americans who had to endure the Depression of the 1930s and World War II. The major events of Greeley's life—and he was often at the center of them—the Depression of 1837, the Mexican War, the divisions of 1850s, the Civil War and Reconstruction, sorely tested Greeley's faith in the dream, yet he did not despair. He had witnessed the ravages of economic dislocation, the misplaced patriotism of an aggressive war, the fury of proslavery advocates, the tragedy of civil conflict, but his flexible mind looked always for solution through democratic processes. Even if his solutions seemed unrealistic and inadequate sometimes, the passion, the excitement were present. Greeley well knew that America never was the innocent Eden some imagined it, but he always believed in the promise. If he were alive today in this era of limits to growth and what historian Henry Steele Commager has called an "Age of No Confidence," he would urge the nation to new elevation.

One of Greeley's great strengths was his style. In his *Recollections*, Greeley noted how as a printer apprentice he learned the advantage of terseness and precision in expression by his experience as a compo-sitor: he had to place individual letters in old trays and keep the words within the limitations of the prescribed page length. As opposed to some of the more obscure pronouncements of men and women whom he admired, like Transcendentalists and other reformers, he had the ability to speak clearly to the hearts and minds of a broad spectrum of literate American men and women—hence his immense popularity and readability. He could take complex issues and treat them with the felicity and simplicity of expression found in forefathers like Paine, Jefferson, and Franklin, with whom he was most often compared.

John G. Shortall affectionately recalled visiting Greeley in his office in 1851:

Sitting at a desk as high as his chin, with his back toward you as you entered, you might have seen [Greeley], his long flaxen hair, curling a little at the ends very thinly covering his large shapely head, the floor about his feet thickly strewn with exchanges, and nothing audible but the scratch, scratch, of that busy pen . . . his gold framed spectacles well upon his forehead, and his chin almost touching the large, white, well-formed hand with which he wrote his almost undecipherable "Copy," sheet after sheet of which he would throw upon the floor beside him, or hold upon his knees. When he turned toward you, however, the curiously shrewd, yet child-like face, cleanshaven, with its sweet smile, and the combination of directness, earnestness, honesty, visible in it, when once well seen, could never be forgotten.[7]

But Greeley had his limits as a thinker, as biographer Glyndon Van Deusen has perceived. While a powerful antislavery advocate, Greeley in his judgment of the quality of black talents was equivocal at best. A strong supporter of public, institutional education, he nonetheless was proud of his informal efforts at self-education. A sponsor of the labor movement, he opposed strikes and labor conflict, advocating cooperation instead. A believer in free will, he rigidly opposed divorce, change in family life-style, and consumption of alcoholic beverages. An advocate of women's rights, he had doubts about women's suffrage. An opponent of capital punishment, he would allow it in some cases. A rationalist, he could accept the possibility of mesmerism. A socialist in his deep concern for the poor, he rejected the major tenets of modern socialism with his support of the principles of capitalism. A supporter of central government authority in such matters as civil rights and internal improvements, he remained deeply suspicious of governmental abuses of power. An advocate of change, he rejected the means of violent revolution. A believer in the new technology, he opposed the vision of a managerial-technocratic elite.

Superficially, Greeley seemed full of ambiguities: a Jeffersonian democrat who belonged to the conservative Whig party, a social reformer who upheld the high tariff, a man of peace who strongly supported wartime conscription, a man of the city who loved farming, a man who celebrated the past and yearned for the future. But there were greater consistency and development in Greeley's thought than such a cursory glance at his positions would indicate. On a number of major issues, he displayed a remarkable and perhaps too rigid consistency: his espousal of Western homesteading, his antislavery stance, his belief in Association.

III   *Editor*

Greeley was born on February 3, 1811, in Amherst, New Hampshire. As a youngster, he knew hardship but never deprivation. His father, Zaccheus, forever engaged in unsuccessful attempts to found a prosperous farm, moved the family continually, from Amherst to Bedford, back to Amherst, then to Westhaven, Vermont in 1825, and to Erie County, Pennsylvania, much to the despair of his mother, Mary Woodburn. Greeley showed a special brilliance in school, gaining a reputation as the best speller in the area. In an 1845 letter to Moses Cortland, to whom Greeley offered an autobiographical sketch, he stressed that besides spelling, reading came easily to him: "I could read very fluently at 4 years of age and quite passable with the book upside down—an absurd practice, which I was stimulated to persist in by those who should have known better. This, too, is the theme of modern fables."[8] He ended his formal education at the age of fourteen.

As he learned the lessons of being constantly uprooted as a youngster, he also was introduced early to his chosen profession when in 1826 he became a printer's apprentice for the *Northern Spectator* of East Poultney. In journalism, he discovered the mainstay of his economic life, as apprentice, printer, reporter, editor, publisher. He later worked for the *Erie Gazette* before removing to New York City where he found some employment in the age of Jackson as a printer for such papers as the *Evening Post*, *The Spirit of the Times* and the *Morning Post*.

Beginning with his apprenticeship, Greeley gradually learned the economy and boldness of style which characterized his best writing. Often his willingness to take a decisive position led to a tenacity which would prove insensitive to the complexity of issues being discussed.

But this could also be a refreshing quality, which enhanced the clarity and energy of his style. Part of the problem behind the disparity between the simplicity of some of his statements and the reality of his more measured thinking came from Greeley's political nature. The clash between image and actuality represented the conflict between power and principle.

From 1831 on, New York City was to be his major residence for the rest of his life, and Greeley's perspective would always be influenced by that growing metropolis. In the years from 1831 to 1872, when he lived there, the city would grow from about 200,000 to over a million residents, and it would become the cultural and fiscal center of the United States.

Greeley's first venture as an editor began with the publication of the *New-Yorker* on March 22, 1834, in partnership with Jonas Winchester. The *New-Yorker* was striking as a Greeley publication because it was nonpartisan, something very different from Greeley's frank espousal of Whiggery in later publications. Also, the *New-Yorker* sponsored literary works as well as the news. The *New-Yorker* proved important to Greeley's career because it gave him his first experience in editorial writing and laid the basis for later positions. Also, Greeley would always remain closely in touch with literary circles in New York City.

After the *New-Yorker* faltered because of the Depression of 1837, Greeley launched into political publication, partially out of dire necessity. He formed a noted "partnership" with William Seward and Thurlow Weed, the famous and powerful Whig leaders of New York state. From this arrangement emerged two publications, the *Jeffersonian*, published from February 17, 1838, to February 17, 1839, and the *Log Cabin*, begun on May 2, 1840, to promote the Whig presidential candidates, William Henry Harrison and John Tyler. Also, Greeley remained a devoted disciple of the famous Whig leader, Henry Clay.

While mourning the death of Harrison on April 4, 1841, Greeley, with Weed's support, issued the first Whig daily paper of New York City on April 10, 1841. With its brilliant staff, exciting editorials, broad coverage of international and national events, the *Tribune* set a new standard for American journalism. Furthermore, its pages were filled with book reviews and excerpts from literary works, absorbing Greeley's interest from the *New-Yorker*. Both the *New-Yorker* and the *Log Cabin* were merged into the *Weekly Tribune* on September 20, 1841; the *Weekly Tribune* would become the national paper for the

Midwest. By the eve of the Civil War, circulation of all issues of the
Tribune—daily, weekly, and semiweekly—approached 300,000
copies. The paper also provided Greeley with a more than adequate
income, although he generously offered to share the ownership of the
paper with his employees in a business transaction in 1850.

Part of Greeley's paper focused on city problems, of course, but his
strength lay in his capacity to pitch the paper's content and editorials
to a national rather just a local audience. Any cursory survey of the
daily *Tribune* still can awe the modern reader with the depth of its
coverage. Open a copy of the *Tribune* from any of the six days (except
on Sunday) it appeared in the 1840s, 1850s, 1860s, and discover in it
full reports of European and national developments, learned commentary, printed government documents, book reviews, remarks on
New York City. The *Tribune* remains to this day an excellent resource
for the history of New York and national politics.

One reason for the *Tribune's* success against such rivals as William
Cullen Bryant's *Evening Post*, James Raymond's *New York Times*,
and James Gordon Bennett's *Herald* was the astonishingly able group
of editors and reporters Greeley gathered about him: Solon Robinson
on agriculture; James S. Pike, Washington correspondent; Bayard
Taylor, the greatest travel writer of his day; Charles Dana, the able
managing editor who would subsequently become assistant secretary
of war and editor of the *New York Sun;* Karl Marx, who, with Freid-
rich Engels's help, composed observations on European affairs in the
1850s and sent them from London; Margaret Fuller, who in the 1840s
wrote brilliant reviews of the works of authors like Edgar Allan Poe
and Charles Brockden Brown and who stayed with the Greeleys in
New York City; and as literary critic after Fuller, George Ripley, the
minister who had been president of Brook Farm. Many of these
remained quite loyal, despite becoming well known for their own
work. Part of this richness of talent was generated by Greeley's
personal magnetism, and part of it came from his great tolerance for a
wide diversity of views.

Greeley's positions in his editorials represented some of the most
important trends of public, social, and political commentary of his
day. In the early 1840s, he strongly supported the reform
movements, from Fourierism to antislavery. He espoused the westward movement and a policy of wide distribution of public lands. As a
congressman, he introduced one of the first homestead bills in Congress in 1848. He opposed the Compromise of 1850, largely because
of the powerful Fugitive Slave Act contained in its provisions. He

denounced the Kansas-Nebraska Bill in 1854, and helped form the Republican party in the same year, when he also declared his political independence of Weed and Seward. He consistently supported the Republican party in the presidential campaigns of 1856 and 1860, although as a delegate to the Chicago convention, he did initially support Edward Bates of Missouri over Abraham Lincoln for the presidential nomination in 1860.

While opposing the secession of South Carolina after Lincoln's election, Greeley counseled against war and argued for the legitimacy of the secessionist principle if it were broadly and democratically supported in a given region; he claimed that South Carolina's act was not popular among the majority of the Southern people. Once war began in 1861, he firmly supported the Northern cause, although he pressed hard for an emancipation edict. While it remains doubtful he influenced Abraham Lincoln in the timing of the Emancipation Proclamation, there is little question that he amassed public opinion behind the document of 1863, conveniently deemphasizing its limitations. While the Army of the Potomac was engaged in its brutal and costly Virginian campaign in the summer of 1864, Greeley involved himself in an abortive attempt to secure peace with self-designated Confederate peace commissioners in Niagara Falls, Ontario. Recovering from that, Greeley abandoned his initial support of Salmon Chase by the fall of 1864.

During Reconstruction, Greeley adopted the stance of universal amnesty and universal suffrage, signed the bail bond of Jefferson Davis in 1867, and by the early 1870s found himself in opposition to President Ulysses Grant and joined the Liberal Republican movement, despite his longtime friendship and correspondence with the vice-president, Schuyler Colfax. In 1872, he became both the Liberal Republican and Democratic standard-bearer, and despite the ridicule of the Republican opponents, he emerged as both a national and distinguished candidate. But Grant's power was strong; the scandals which would plague his second Administration had not yet fully surfaced. Greeley was crushed in the general election, and saddened both by this loss and his wife's death a few days before election day, Greeley died on November 29, 1872. Hence, his public life sadly met disappointment in the pursuit of ultimate power; part of the problem lay with Greeley's own ambition for office. Like Abraham Lincoln, Greeley continually tried and failed at various elections, except for his three-month term as a congressman from 1848 to 1849.

Instead, if Greeley had been content to nurture his own paper and editorship, his career would have been termed an astounding success. But, in certain ways, his search for power grew out of the distinctive way in which he fashioned his image as editor of the *Tribune*. He wanted to be the voice of the people, as one biographer, William Harlan Hale, astutely noted. He loved crowds, and he courted fame assiduously. Both Ralph Waldo Emerson and Henry David Thoreau noted with disapproval how Greeley was often surrounded by people, and Greeley seemed to enjoy the good humor people made out of his eccentricities, from his ungainly appearance to the illegibility of his writing. That Greeley should seek the presidency should surprise no one familiar with the public image he chose to court.

Hence Greeley cultivated his image as "everyman," speaking out against those who would corrupt and misuse the people's trust. What was admirable about Greeley, despite the susceptibility he showed to his own "fame" and "fortune," was the continued independence of his positions. However unpopular and at times ridiculous these positions were, they were unique and often constructive, such as his opposition to the abuse of the franking privilege and travel expenses in Congress and his concern for peace in the terrible summer of 1864 during the war. One may not always respect Greeley's opinions and vacillations, but one cannot avoid liking the man.

Throughout Greeley's life, there were a number of episodes which through his own humorous accounts he made notorious: his clash with James Fenimore Cooper over a libel suit in 1842 which he dubbed the "Cooperism" of the *Tribune;* his controversial printed exchange with Henry J. Raymond over Fourierism in 1846–1847; his two-day incarceration on a visit to Paris in 1855 over a complaint from his directorship of the New York Exposition of 1853; his interview with Brigham Young in Utah in 1859 where he challenged Young's commitments to polygamy and slavery; his famous dispute with Robert Dale Owen over the legitimacy of divorce.

At one point, Greeley visited Washington during the winter of 1855–1856, ostensibly to help in the fight to elect a Republican to the House speakership—the candidate, Nathaniel Banks, was subsequently triumphant. However, because of his adamant position, Greeley invited the ire of Democratic politicos, so much so that Congressman Albert Rust of Arkansas caned him on the capital streets. Unlike Charles Sumner's poor physical condition after the assault by Preston Brooks, Greeley emerged unscathed and would later make merry with the incident in the *Recollections*.

In his 1851 travelogue, *Glances at Europe*, Greeley related his adventures as a jury chairman at the American exposition at the London World's Fair held in the Crystal Palace and as a continental tourist. In England, he reported on conversations with such noted reformers as Richard Cobden and how he explained the American antislavery movement to British audiences. He left Europe with a renewed appreciation for American culture. He defended the treasures of American art by denouncing the "self-constituted arbiter who . . . tell the American people that Art is not their province—that they should be content to grow Corn and Cotton. . . . Are they not palpably speaking in the interest of the rival producers of Europe, alarmed by the rapid growth and extension of American Art?" He finished his work with a prose hymn:

Hark! the last gun announces that the mail-boat has left us, and that we are fairly afloat on our ocean journey: the shores of Europe recede from our vision; the watery waste is all around us; and now, with God above and Death below, our gallant bark her clustered company together brave the dangers of the mighty deep. May Infinite Mercy watch over our onward path and bring us safely to our several homes; for to die away from home and kindred seems one of the saddest calamities that could befall me![9]

On occasion, he displayed enormous courage, particularly when he carried on the business of the *Tribune* when the *Tribune* building was attacked by rioters in early July 1863 because of the paper's strong support of conscription. He overcame early adversity: for example, the death from drowning of Francis V. Story in 1834, the burning of the *New-Yorker* office in 1835 and of the *Tribune* building in 1845.

Despite his public optimism, Greeley showed the dread, the doubt which so haunted the nineteenth century. Part of this undoubtedly came from the tragic dimensions of Greeley's personal life. For he had seen his parents' lives end in unhappiness in Western Pennsylvania. His marriage to Mary Cheney in 1836, begun initially with much promise, soon lapsed into a strained relationship which resulted partially from his wife's ill health. He lost five of seven children, including his own beloved son, "Pickie." He certainly could have endorsed Thomas Hardy's phrase, "happiness is but the occasional episode in a general drama of pain."

Greeley also had disagreeable traits. He could be irrascible and tough on both opponents and subordinates. As Pennsylvania politico, A. K. McClure, stated, Greeley "was an intense hater, and often misjudged men when he became prejudiced against them."[10] Working for Greeley could not have always been easy, as he was at times disorganized and irritable. Because of personal disagreements, Greeley summarily dismissed his able assistant, Charles Dana, in 1862, despite fifteen years of expert service. He complained constantly over the paper's appearance and content when he was traveling and hence not in immediate control of the office. He was notorious for the poor quality of his penmanship, which caused both his printers and countless modern researchers many moments of despair as they sought to decipher his illegible prose. Mark Twain, who worked briefly for the *Tribune* in the late 1860s, made fun of Greeley's scratchings in *Roughing It*. Greeley could be obstinate and petty at times. His letter announcing to Thurlow Weed and William Seward the end of their powerful Whig partnership in 1854 was filled with trivial animosities and reads poorly in retrospect. His opposition to Seward's presidential candidacy in 1860 seemed motivated more by personal resentment than by principle.

As Glyndon Van Deusen has noted, Greeley was not a fully devoted family man. His heavy newspaper commitments, political obligations, and constant traveling caused him to neglect some of his domestic duties, and while he deeply loved his wife and two daughters, Ida and Gabrielle, he did not devote much time to them. Part of his disregard undoubtedly stemmed from his disappointment over the death of "Pickie"; part of it came from his wife's complaining nature. Clearly, the pretty and bright Mary Cheney grew pale to Greeley's eyes as he grew older, yet often he had only himself to blame for a strained marriage.

Indeed, Greeley remained somewhat of an enigma in personality. After breaking with Weed and Seward, he had no really close friends; he remained strangely isolated.

Yet what gave grace to even Greeley's worst foibles was his own honesty about them, his good cheer about life's struggles, his dignified conduct, his amazing willingness to converse with anyone about national and local issues. If he remained closed about his inner being, his public self was fully open. Even in correspondence, Greeley rarely spoke solely with a private voice; he always commented on public issues and took stances often remarkably consistent with those in his published works.

Despite personal problems and its tragic end, Greeley's life was a rich one, and if he were busy and hard working, he was essentially happy in his professional existence. He lived most of his adult life in one of the exciting cities in the world. He was able to establish himself in a fine location as the first "suburbanite" in the lovely woods of

Chappaqua. Despite abundant commitments in New York City, he journeyed widely through much of the United States, South and North, and throughout Europe. And besides his principal role as editor of the greatest national newspaper of his day, the *Weekly Tribune*, known as a "political Bible" for many, he had experience as a farmer, politician, literary critic, delegate, reform leader. He had access to most of the major leaders of his time. In his journal, Ralph Waldo Emerson noted that "I think Horace Greeley's career one of the most encouraging facts in our Whiggish age. A white-haired man in the city of New York has adopted every benevolent crotchet and maintained it, until he commands an army of a million now in the heart of the United States."[11] That such a poor, strange looking lad could rise to such power and prestige was a testament to the nineteenth-century belief in success and progress.

Of course, he had accomplished much. The histories of American journalism, American reform, American nationalism, American politics are the richer for him. And he was honored. The testimonies of countless letters from the youth of the country underscored his influence. For example, after his death, one of his associates, J. C. Forman, testified that from

my youth, beginning with the New Yorker, and afterwards with the first number of the New Tribune . . . I have been familiar with the writings of Mr. Greeley, almost always agreeing with him in his opinions and convictions, and admiring the earnestness, vigor and clearness with which he advocated what he believed to be the cause of truth, and the rights and welfare of mankind.[12]

In one of the major references to Greeley's famous phrase, "Go West, young man," the influential Iowa clergyman who founded Grinnell College, Josiah Bushnell Grinnell, recalled how Greeley gave him the advice of the century: when Grinnell, suffering from poor health, made his way to the *Tribune* offices one day, Greeley told him not to "lounge in the city. . . . Go West, young man, go West. There is health in the country, and room away from our crowds of idlers and imbeciles." To aid Grinnell, Greeley assigned him to report for the *Tribune* on the activities of the Illinois State Fair at Springfield. In this fashion, Greeley underwrote a new life for Grinnell: "I was the young man whom Mr. Greeley told to go, and I went."[13] However, Greeley's phrase did not necessarily imply a pastoral bias; in many ways, he was advising young people to go out to the provinces of America, but not necessarily back to farming.

In presenting his version of a homestead bill, Greeley showed that he had concrete procedures to support his encouragement of young people to go West. Again, he emphasized his belief in an American nationalism which not only allowed for the possession of rights, but which provided means to fulfill those rights. It was not enough to espouse the right to property, should one have the good fortune to possess it; the nation-state should guarantee to each citizen fair means of acquiring property. Greeley claimed his bill as the "only [one] to recognize . . . the principle that a man is entitled to live *somewhere,* although he has no money wherewith to buy land to live on . . . while [the bill] guards the interests of the whole country, it secures a home to every one who will claim it, without money and without price."[14] The specific provisions of the bill did not quite sustain Greeley's full generalization, but it anticipated many features of the Homestead Act of 1862. While referring to the traditional quartered section of land, the bill authorized any individuals who settle on a quarter-section to preempt forty acres without charge should he build a home on those acres within seven years.

Greeley never forgot the help of others, especially when the Depression of 1837 hit, the "evil days," as he called them. His files are filled with letters advising the young, serving as references, and occasionally offering money. For instance, at one point, he helped Henry David Thoreau have his pieces published.

Greeley's policy as editor eschewed sensationalism and even reporting of sporting events at first; what was refreshing about his attitude was that he did not actively cater to his audience. He was not a Citizen Kane. Rather, he wished to establish a forum for free exchange of ideas, no matter how blatantly stated.

Greeley lives in his writing, the ultimate source of his power, and one only needs to open again his *Recollections,* peruse his editorials, hear in the mind's ear some of his best lectures, and read portions of his Civil War history, *The American Conflict,* to rediscover the fire which so stirred the nation. Greeley in his best moments was an educator to people, and he still has much to say. Experiencing Greeley's writing today opens the way to the power of nineteenth-century America, and suddenly that century lives again, with its color, majesty, faith, and optimism, when the American providence seemed young, bouyant, and immemorial.

CHAPTER 2

The Editor

H ORACE Greeley was one of the great editorial writers in Ameri-can history; in this short form, Greeley found the proper format in which he could compose passages of persuasive force. Clearly his background as a printer and craftsman helped shape his editorial style. He recalled in the *Recollections* that he had learned as an apprentice how to "give in fewer words the gist of . . . informa-tion. . . . The rudimentary knowledge of the art of composition thus acquired was gradually improved during my brief experience as a journeyman in various newspaper establishments."[1] The hurried quality, the occasional obtuseness of his longer, formal works, whether book, lectures, or articles, were absent in the editorials; here, under the discipline of the exacting spatial dimensions of the newspaper, Greeley's language successfully evoked the passion of his ideas.

I *The Power of Words*

If Greeley continually failed in his quest for political power, he succeeded in cultivating another kind of power, the power over the mind. While Greeley could employ scolding tactics in his editorial prose, at the same time his best efforts retain spark and remain remarkably balanced and judicious in comment. Compared with editorials found in most American newspapers today, Greeley's were superior in incisive comment, intellectual challenge, diction, effec-tive analysis. Of course, Greeley had the advantage of being able to present a single vision; while today's editorials usually form a compo-site and compromise of varying views, Greeley could and did give his own opinion, often unhampered by political considerations for other dissenting views among the staff. Also, Greeley had the license to be bold about his political ties, at first Whig and then Republican; he did not feel the need to be nonpartisan. Such were the habits of nine-teenth-century personal journalism.

To modern readers, some of Greeley's editorials may seem offensive because of a didactic tendency, but this existed because Greeley saw himself as teacher as well as commentator; the role of the editor was to serve as public educator as well as advocate, to provide essential information to enable readers to make measured judgments. Therefore, Greeley would often trace the history behind a crisis to provide a framework for his ideas. A selective study of Greeley's best editorials reveals two significant points: first, some of his most important ideas, like his commitment to Western settlement and his faith in communitarian enterprises, emerged in his earliest editorials; second, he never lost the stylistic strength of his earliest work.

For instance, Greeley supported the twin principles of universal suffrage and universal amnesty during Reconstruction in the late 1860s, as did many others, but his support of universal suffrage was long-standing. In the *Jeffersonian* in 1838, Greeley had identified universal suffrage as an essential element for democracy. With this commitment would come the necessity of universal education. Greeley dreamed of a "consolidation of government of reason and law through the necessary diffusion of Intelligence. But in establishing Universal suffrage as the cornerstone of our political fabric, we stand morally pledged to use every means within the power of the State to accompany it by Universal Education." His call for the black franchise was central to his democratic credo. In an 1846 editorial, he stated that unless

it can be shown that all White men are virtuous and competent to pass judgment on great questions of State, and that no Black men are so—(and surely no man ever did or could pretend this)—then it is clear that a Constitutional denial to Black men, as such, of Political Rights freely secured to White men, is monstrously unjust and irrational.[2]

What distinguished Greeley's prose was its clarity; he could marshall his words in a direct march toward a specific objective. He would recognize the arguments of the opposition and then disarm them. When he reached his conclusion, no other seemed possible. Of course, this approach meant that Greeley dismissed certain subtleties, sometimes consciously. The rhythm of Greeley's prose alternated between the quiet, conversational tone and the loud, militant, oratorical.

Greeley was always fascinated with words. One contemporary observed that, as a youth, he was always "at the head of the school. His spelling was the talk for miles around. I remember of his missing a word just once. His face turned red, and he was silent for a moment; then he broke forth loud enough for all to hear, 'What a fool!'" Greeley had devoted the *New-Yorker* to literature, and much of the space of the *Tribune* was set aside for literary reviews, book notices, serializing novels. Ironically, Greeley in the early days of the *Tribune* remained devoted to poetry over prose. In a personal letter, he said rather cynically that prose "is not worth writing, except for bread. To live it must be Poetry, only unmarked by Rhyme." Greeley made some attempts at poetry, albeit not too successfully. In a tribute to Ireland in 1843, entitled "Ode for the Meetings of the Friends of Ireland," Greeley's concluding lines captured both the spirit and rather conventional style of the piece,

> On the trail of their legions no ashes are seen,
> No captive is shackled, no slave bends the knee;
> All Earth's be the joy, hers the verdure of green,
> But the glory, O Erin, shall linger with thee.

Despite his misgivings, in prose Greeley discovered the right medium. An editorial memorializing Greeley upon his death in 1872 succinctly summarized Greeley's effectiveness, "As a writer, he was vigorous, lucid and convincing; not always polished yet always forcible."[3]

Central to Greeley's editorial style was his belief that only an open forum of competing ideas could provide foundations for democracy. Hence he believed deeply in the press. In an editorial in the *Jeffersonian,* Greeley stated that the "Power without knowledge, and, what is worse, without Principle, . . . [would] subvert our liberties." Like John Adams, he saw a free press as an essential control over the conduct of the powerful. Said Adams, "The Public safety demands efficient extension of Knowledge to the ultimate limits of Power." Elsewhere, Greeley declared that the

Liberty of the Press is the palladium of all true Liberty; with it despotism is impossible, without it inevitable. Evil triumphs . . . because the few are rendered powerful by intelligence, concert, and the command of material resources, while the many are paralyzed by ignorance, disunion and poverty. That a majority should persist in perpetuating injustice, after a full and free discussion, is scarcely tolerable as hypothesis, and wholly unjustified by facts.

"With a Free Press for twenty years in Russia and South Carolina," Greeley boldly declaimed, "the former would establish a Republic, and the latter abolish her Slavery."[4]

Greeley's first biographer, James Parton, stressed how Greeley believed in a free press as a "cheap press." Only by offering a paper for as small a sum as possible, could it be readily available to all. Hence the first issue of the daily *Tribune* on April 10, 1841, cost only one penny. Said Parton, the inexpensive press could unite the national community: "It makes this huge commonwealth, else so heterogeneous and disunited, think with one mind, feel with one heart, and talk with one tongue."[5]

II *Commentary on Slavery*

Greeley's editorials reflected some of the most incisive, measured commentary responding to the most important crisis in American history since the Revolution. They struck the initial hope of the era of reform in the 1830s before the Depression of 1837, and then the yielding of all reform movements to the antislavery crusade of the 1840s and 1850s, ending in the subversion of peace and then recovery.

A good example of his special editorial power can be found in an 1846 statement on the nation's independence. Here, in a convincing rhetorical style typical of the abolitionists, Greeley pitted the nation's ideals against current realities, the perpetuation of slavery and the prosecution of the Mexican War. Greeley critiqued "another sort of patriotism" which would overlook ugliness because to "flatter and please is the easier, more agreeable course." Greeley argued that a greater patriotism than that of "ear tinkling" Fourth of July orations would be the "stern task of proclaiming the naked and useful Truth!" Greeley displayed his balanced approach by attacking both the South and the North in the treatment of black Americans. In "defiance of the National Creed," said Greeley, Southern states "authorize a part of their People to hold the residue in bondage through life, to force them to unrequited labor by the . . . application of the lash and to sell the children from the mothers, the husband from the wife, in hapless, life long separation." The North merited Greeley's wrath for its inconsistency between democratic ideals and segregationist realities:

These are equally unfaithful in principle. . . . Here, in the midst of our Democratic equality . . . we . . . sustain an Aristocracy of Color more rigid and hateful than any Aristocracy known to the Old World. We, the rampant Democrats of America, with our mouths full of lying cant about Equality, Justice and the area of Freedom, banish the children of Africa from our public conveyances, from our civic convocations, and even from a practical equality as sinners in our assemblages to supplicate the mercy of God![6]

Greeley then invoked dissent from the Mexican War in a fashion reminiscent of Henry David Thoreau's essay on civil disobedience two years later; this "horrible War is another instance of gross infidelity to the principles which made us a Nation.—We are fighting not to preserve Liberty but to perpetuate Slavery—not in defence of our own territory but in encroachment on that of our feeblest neighbor." Greeley generalized from the specific to embrace the cause of social justice. He argued that as long as poverty like that represented by slavery existed in America, so long did the country defy the natural philosophy of its Revolutionary heritage:

Every child growing up in ignorance; every youth groping his way through Idleness, Want, physical or mental, to Shame and Crime; every parent who, having done his best to procure by honest toil and the means of subsistence, goes home to face his hungry children or trembles for the destitution which threatens and approaches them, justly accuses this People of unfaithfulness to the great and good principles proclaimed at the birth of the first American Republic, which ought to be the protector, monitor and pattern of all her younger sisters but, having fallen behind them in regard to Slavery, is becoming their terror and scourge.[7]

Basic to Greeley's opposition to slavery was his firm belief in free labor. To Greeley, the American revolution was incomplete because while it provided for great political flexibility, it did not eradicate the curse of poverty. This would remain a consistent theme throughout his career. Without freedom from want, intellectual development, so central to national purpose and security, was impossible. Slavery was cursed because it condemned millions to penury. Yet, by the same reasoning, the South as a whole was to be pitied after the Civil War because it was poor, and millions of both whites and blacks were condemned to peasantry. Greeley wanted more for poor Americans than mere opportunity to compete; he wanted a change in power structures to make jobs guaranteed to all. This was why with his friend Arthur Brisbane he embraced Fourierism, or Association, as he called it, so readily in the 1840s. As he stated in a letter to O. H. Bowen, "I have one great hope for Humanity . . . the emancipation of the Children of Want, and . . . Misery, whether in bondage or nominally free, by means of *Association*."[8]

Greeley had been deeply affected by the poverty he saw and felt in New York City in the Depression of 1837–1838, and he wanted to erase such calamities from the American scene. One reason for his support of the westward movement was his hope that available land could be distributed to the needy. He always supported land reform. Long before he became famous for the phrase "Go West, young man," in the early 1850s, he was pressing the theme in the 1830s. In the *New-Yorker*, prior to the Depression, he spoke of the country's prosperity: in the West, "the signs of rude husbandry are quickly displayed, and they in turn succeeded by the hum of rising villages, the hiss of countless steamboats, and the bustle, the varied enterprise, and the unceasing improvement, which mark the origin of American civilization."[9]

Some of Greeley's most powerful editorials responded to the crises of the 1850s. Greeley detested the newly strengthened Fugitive Slave Act from the Compromise of 1850. He termed it "an exactment that cannot stand and be executed in the non-slaveholding states." When it was passed in 1850, it wore "the aspect of a compromise between rival sections, essential to the preservation of national harmony." But to Greeley, by 1854, the realities of 1850 had changed in four years for the "slave states have hoisted the banner of aggression upon Freedom." Here, Greeley railed against the Kansas-Nebraska Bill, which, with its provisions for popular sovereignty, could open the West to slavery. With the passage of the act, which also repealed the Missouri Compromise arranged by the beloved Clay, Greeley recognized that "to many" these were rare hours "of discouragement," for there was "rejoicing around the auction-blocks of Richmond, the slave-pews of Charleston, and a wilder revelry in the midnight orgies of the dealers in human sinews generally, at the prospect of new markets opening for their merchandise at once in the South and in the West." But Greeley exalted his readers to persevere. For the "turn" of the antislavery crusade would come:

For this is not an age of the world in which new domain can be opened to slavedrivers without an instinctive shudder convulsing the frame of Humanity. . . . The stars in their course fight against the further enslavement and brutalization of the terrestrial image of God. . . . And, whatever may be the issue of the immediate struggle we will unswervingly trust that the forces are silently maturing which shall rid our land . . . of the scandal and crime of the enslaving and auctioneering the countrymen of Washington and Jefferson.

Said Greeley earlier, we "are in the midst of revolution. . . . The attempted passage of this measure is the first great effort of Slavery to take American freedom directly by the throat."[10]

An 1854 editorial comparing the domestic slave trade with a possible renewal of the African trade featured the best and worst of

Greeley's crusading spirit. Like Southern apologists for slavery, Greeley believed that an enforced transfer to America would benefit the "wild, brutal African," because he "would be carried off to a truly religious and cultivated country." While Greeley showed unwelcome bias against African culture, he could eloquently sympathize with American blacks: "to the native of Virginia or Maryland there is no greater calamity than that of being torn from the home of his childhood and the objects of his affection in order to be 'sold South.'"[11]

Greeley deeply opposed what he saw as the conspiratorial nature of the Dred Scott decision. In reference to John Brown, Greeley displayed a balanced view as he praised Brown's goals but condemned his violent methods. In 1860, he hoped for Republican victory, which had been denied in 1856.

Even when Greeley needlessly exaggerated, he could be effective. In commemorating George Washington on his birthday on February 22, 1864, Greeley confronted the dilemma central to the heritage of the Union now actively fighting a war for freedom, that the Founders were slaveholders themselves. His conclusion, claiming "Washington an Emancipationist," was certainly unjustified by facts, but his full presentation was judicious. He noted how the "Abolition of Slavery was first suggested by Virginian statesmen, who were themselves slaveholders." He criticized Southern claims to Washington as supporting the cause of slavery: "These men were nearer the infancy of the Republic than we are—they knew what doctrines of human equality the revolution was intended to vindicate and establish—they felt, as we can never feel, the pressure of strictly logical conclusions."[12] He cataloged Washington's views on slavery; it was immoral, evil for both master and slave. Greeley stressed how Washington had manumitted many of his slaves in his will.

As secession seemed more imminent with Lincoln's election, no editorial was more controversial than Greeley's statement about letting the Southern states go. Yet Greeley, like both Charles Sumner and Abraham Lincoln, tried to resolve a conflict embedded in the American reform heritage, between the right of revolution and the perpetuity of the Union, between the commitment to freedom and the commitment to peace. Greeley clearly did not want war, yet he had raised a militant banner against slavery. He believed deeply in genuine revolutionary movements, yet he loved American nationhood. As Thomas Bonner has noted, if the Southern movement represented a true democracy, Greeley was prepared to recognize the legitimacy of its independence. But he placed severe qualifications on the secessionist movement. He doubted it had the support of the majority of the white people, much less the blacks. He questioned the Southern claim on the heritage of the Founders. He had constantly ridiculed the South's notions of aristocracy, privilege, economic despotism. To him, it represented a closed, callous society. But at the same time, he could not bear to "live in a republic whereby one section is joined to the residue by bayonets."[13]

In an editorial a few weeks after the election of 1860, Greeley argued persuasively that the vote in the South was not necessarily pro-secessionist. Yet, too eagerly, he discounted the secessionist threat. In his entry of November 28, 1860, he argued that even if South Carolina would take steps—and here he still had doubts—he felt that other "Calhoun states," such as Georgia, Alabama, Mississippi, and Florida, would not follow the lead. As he said, "We believe [South Carolina] will not leap into the gulf of Disunion alone, but, when she reaches its brink, will wait for the countenance and cooperation of Sister States. Will they join her, and go down with her?" Here he argued that the broad sentiment of the people was for Union: "In all of [these states] with the exception of South Carolina, probably a majority of the people are at heart opposed to withdrawing from the Union . . . for any such reasons as have yet been announced." Despite this Greeley's Calvinist suspicions were prevalent:

When madness rules the hour, calculations based upon the reasonableness of men are ofttimes very much at fault. The Secession leaders are bent upon precipitating their scheme ere "the sober second thought" of the rural population can make itself felt in restraining the headlong movement. Impelled to action by a foregone purpose, these leaders did not stop to calculate consequences. They have succeeded in turning the popular current in these five States toward disunion. It may sweep them to a point where retreat is impossible, and thus carry both the willing and unwilling over the precipice into the chasm.[14]

But Greeley could be adamant about his own support of the Union. While he had been critical of national compromises, most notably the Compromise of 1850, Greeley had always endorsed compromise as a necessary ingredient in the democratic process. His objections to Senator John Crittenden's proposed compromise on the eve of Civil War, essentially to extend the Mason-Dixon line into Western territory, represented the mood of much of the North as to why compromise was no longer possible in America. In an open letter, Greeley stated the case for Union. The Southern challenge denied American principles of restraint of power, of free speech, of free press, of peaceful democracy. Mob rule was rampant. No compromise would resolve this; only Northern strict adherence to principle would prevail. Here again, Greeley looked to power for good. He based his argument on the American principle of the supremacy of law, what he termed the "majesty of law" over the arbitrary whims of men. He feared that the secessionist challenge so disrupted the electoral process that the United States might sink into a chaos which invited dictatorships. He called for "unbroken peace and prosperity" and worried that "the system established by our fathers [could] give place to one of South American . . . revolts by the defeated in each election." He argued that while one state prosecuted "open rebellion against the Federal authority," there could be no talk of compromise. Furthermore, while the Compromise of 1850 demanded that the North surrender Louisiana, Florida, and Texas to slavery, it would not sacrifice "Freedom" in New Mexico and Arizona.[15] Greeley claimed that many in the South would not accept the Crittenden Compromise and that no one in the North would be allowed the free speech and press to preach their case in the South.

III   *Civil War and Reconstruction*

Greeley contributed vitally to the debate over emancipation during the Civil War. He crystallized the disappointment of many antislavery advocates when he called upon President Lincoln to free the slaves under the provisions of the second Confiscation Act in one of his most famous editorials, that of August 20, 1862. Certainly the style of this piece did not match the eloquence of Lincoln's famous reply of August 22 that his "paramount object in this struggle is to save the Union, and is not to either save or destroy slavery," but Greeley's message was cleverly framed. He reminded the president of his sworn duty to "execute the laws," and he asked that Lincoln enforce the law's provisions to authorize commanders to free all slaves of masters engaged in rebellious actions. Said Greeley, those "provisions were designed to fight Slavery with Liberty." He dismissed Lincoln's sensitivity to the case of the loyal border states where slavery was still legal by urging Lincoln to give heart to those areas of the South where the principle of free labor was paramount. Lincoln had temporized with slavery at home, left it alone in conquered areas, and refused to strengthen its foes in the South. The army, supposedly engaged on a march to freedom, instead was an ally to slavery when many of its commanders refused to accept slaves within their lines. Hence an effective instrument of power for good was blunted. Furthermore, like many others, Greeley rebuked Lincoln

for overturning General John C. Fremont's and General David
Hunter's proclamations of local emancipation. Referring to slavery as
the cause of war, Greeley closed with eloquence:

As one of the millions who would gladly have avoided this struggle at any
sacrifice but that of Principle and Honor, but who now feel that the triumph of
the Union is indispensable not only to the existence of our country but to the
well-being of mankind, I entreat you to render a hearty and unequivocal
obedience to the law of the land.[16]

There has been much debate over how much Greeley's editorial
actually prodded Lincoln into issuing the Preliminary Emancipation
Proclamation of September 22, 1862. This document emphasized the
doctrine of military necessity, as Greeley had, but lacked Greeley's
commitment to the ideology of freedom. The Preliminary Proclamation asserted that all slaves in areas still in rebellion on January 1,
1863, would be free. Historian John Hope Franklin has convincingly
demonstrated that in terms of power, the checking of General Robert
E. Lee at Antietam provided the opportunity for the release of the
Preliminary Proclamation more than Greeley's inquiry had and that
Lincoln had already presented a draft version to his Cabinet on July
22. However, that Greeley was able to engage the president in
elevated public debate illustrated his power as editor.

Greeley responded to Lincoln on August 24 by stating that he
never doubted Lincoln's devotion to the Union. On the basis of
nationalism, however, Greeley asked Lincoln to enforce the second
Confiscation Act. He disputed Lincoln's desire to restore the "Union
as it was" as a hopeless retreat to a past where the Union was not
firmly linked with freedom. Only if "slavery is to be vanquished . . .
by liberty" would their children read "history . . . irradiated by the
glory of national salvation, not rendered lurid by the blood-red glow
of national conflagration and ruin."[17] Here Greeley anticipated what
Lincoln would express so well in the Gettysburg Address and second
inaugural. As the War became a fully modern war, the very nature of
the nation being defended was changing from an open community
which tolerated dissent from its ideals in terms of institutions like
slavery to a mighty power which demanded freedom.

While Greeley clearly was an irritant to Lincoln's steady purpose,
however flexible his means, Lincoln must have found sustenance in
Greeley's instructive support of the final Emancipation Proclamation. In an editorial of January 1, the day of the Proclamation's
issuance, Greeley absolved Lincoln of any charges of opportunism or
indifference concerning the slavery issue. He stated that Lincoln did

not wait until a major military victory to issue the Proclamation. He praised the president's fairness in issuing the document after he had announced only his intention to do so in the Preliminary Proclamation. Also, Greeley countered the charge that Lincoln cared only for the Union and not slavery by admonishing his readers that Lincoln opposed slavery as a person, while his public options were limited:

He has no 'moral nor legal right to assail [slavery] officially on any other ground than that of its proved incompatibility with the salvation of the republic. If he were to decree its overthrow on the ground of its essential cruelty and wickedness, the decree would be invalid. He has no *right* to crush it on any other ground than that of its implacable and dangerous hostility to the National life.[18]

Furthermore, Greeley dismissed the argument that the Proclamation would unite the South; instead it would divide the South by aligning its four million blacks to the Union cause. The Proclamation would not increase the hatred of whites any more than the alleged "atrocities" of the rebels against Union soldiers had already done; in a typically exaggerated but effective catalog, Greeley cited two incidents of "Rebel" savagery: at Bull Run, rebel soldiers had made "rings and other trinkets" out of the "dug up" bones of Union soldiers; in Arkansas they had fled "scalded and shrieking" soldiers in the aftermath of the explosion of a steamboat.[19] Actually, Southern resistance was strongest when the administration was equivocating on the question of slavery.

Greeley stressed the equity of Lincoln's experimental style. Echoing the spirit of Lincoln's letter to him, Greeley said that Lincoln waited until he became convinced that the "Union must be saved at the expense of Slavery or it could not be saved at all."[20] Only when he became so persuaded did he issue the Proclamation.

Greeley noted how dissenters abroad had criticized the Union for the futility of "crushing" the South, whether the Union supported or opposed slavery. Rather than listen to such voices, "we must be guided by our own judgment and conscience, fighting the fight that has been thrust upon us as best we may, leaving results to God." At the same time, Greeley stressed how the new policy would enlist supporters like "Victor Hugo, Garibaldi, John Bright," men who had waited in vain for American idealism to triumph.[21] In short, the Proclamation had enhanced America's cause abroad, as it was now linked with European movements of national liberation.

The Proclamation had contained a clause warning slaves to desist in attempts to commit insurrection but had simultaneously welcomed free blacks into the Union armed forces, in a sense disinviting blacks from forms of illegal violence but encouraging them to join government sanctioned conflict. Unlike the Proclamation, Greeley showed deep concern for the treatment of blacks in Union armies and navies. In a statement representative of a mixture of paternalism and compassion, Greeley asked for a humane and just treatment of the blacks, for they would "prove immensely serviceable to us in many ways, even though we should never own a regiment of them." Greeley saw them in effective roles as spies. Greeley distrusted Northern prejudice, something about which the black abolitionist Frederick Douglas would bitterly complain in a famous interview with Lincoln the following summer. Said Greeley, "the Union Guards and soldiers can still [repel] and [abuse] the Blacks; there is power nowhere else on earth to defeat us. Only let the slaves *feel* that our triumph is their liberation, and they become from that hour a burden instead of a bulwark to the Rebellion."[22]

In an aside which did him no honor, Greeley criticized the blacks for doing "nearly as much to sustain the Rebellion as the Whites; let them realize that to work for their masters is to work for Slavery and Against their own Liberty." In a distasteful comment illustrating Greeley's own limitations, he asked that they "be watched, and guarded, and overawed, and hurried away from the neighborhood of our troops, with an occasional hanging or burning of a refractory one, to make them goodnatured and docile until the Rebellion must collapse."[23]

Despite these statement smacking of the very prejudice which Greeley in his better moments condemned, this editorial displayed the magic of Greeley's style. He showed himself as the public man, aware of many of the arguments over emancipation, yet who could still sound close enough to be in the same room discussing public affairs at the country store. He took on the guise of what commentator Richard Sennett has defined as the "public man" before the fall. He anticipated the critics and disarmed them; he both proclaimed and yielded to conversation. He succumbed to Northern prejudice yet condemned it. His presentation was political because he said something to each of varied regional and ethnic groups: Union soldiers, blacks, abolitionists, unionists. He showed skill in uniting potentially divisive lines of argument.

In many ways, Greeley, once so critical of the Lincoln administration over emancipation policy, became its spokesperson. One must recall that at heart Greeley, like Lincoln, was a nationalist before anything else, and his vision of the national destiny, like Lincoln's, entailed freedom for all. In this and other editorials on the issue, he could move beyond the strictly legal and militaristic trappings of the Proclamation, what historian Richard Hofstadter termed a "bill of lading," and become eloquent; he could overlook its rather severe limitations and declare it to be a document of universal freedom. He could without doubt support the Union cause with more fervor than ever. And despite his paternalism, Greeley foresaw what blacks would also proclaim, that the Proclamation by itself meant little; what counted was what whites and blacks made of it.

Greeley's study of Reconstruction showed much intelligence. In an 1867 editorial, Greeley again called for the universal suffrage linked with universal amnesty, a proposal which had been circulating through Congress as the "Stewart plan." Both ex-Confederates and blacks should be enfranchised. Greeley warned that if during Reconstruction "Rebels" and "Negroes" were denied "any voice in making, amending or executing the laws whereby they are to be governed— who does not know that a new and fierce struggle for their enfranchisement will commence directly." In the interest of peace, Greeley wished to avoid future confrontations. In an editorial entitled "The True Basis of Reconstruction," Greeley, as Lincoln had, showed new respect for blacks. He asked that new laws "treat him as a man" by disregarding the "circumstance of his color and [treating] him only as a human being." This was the way to take the "negro out of politics." Greeley opposed intelligence tests on the grounds that blacks had never had the opportunity to learn. In an eloquent testimonial, Greeley said that

in a state where each child grows up within sight of free school-houses wherein he is more than welcome as a pupil, it is perfectly reasonable to prescribe that those only who can read may vote. Where half the people have not only been denied all public facilities for education but have grown up under laws which made teaching them a crime, the case is very different. Do not put out a man's eyes and then punish him for blindness.

Greeley preached against leaving the blacks at the mercy of the Southern white power structure. Through their active participation in the war, blacks had earned their place in the nation. They had risen above Southern sectionalism to become nationalists:

The Blacks are a portion not merely of the Southern but of the American people. They played an important [role] . . . in our great Civil War. We cannot ignore the obligations springing from . . . their loyalty. I hold that honor and good faith absolutely constrain those who triumphed in that struggle to take care that their humble supporters . . . shall not be made to suffer for taking the side of the Union.

Said Greeley, the North must protect blacks, "no matter what the cost."[24]

Greeley's attitudes toward Reconstruction underlined the symmetry of his thought. The man of peace offered ex-Confederates a second chance; the man of liberty insisted on full black involvement in the political process. When these two aims, peace and freedom, conflicted during the secessionist crisis, Greeley, after some vacillation, chose war. Now he saw the opportunity for reconciliation between his ideals.

During the conflict, Greeley had anticipated the promise of postwar reconstruction. In two Fourth of July editorials, Greeley assessed the impact of the war on the nation. In a July Fourth editorial in 1862, Greeley stressed how the country suffered because in a "furious Civil War" which had "decimated" the American people, "the vultures of Aristocracy and Despotism [are] gathering and circling impatiently for the expected feast on the remains of what was once their chief terror." In an Independence Day editorial written in the midst of the New York City riots, Greeley summed up both the triumph and tragedy of the war. He noted that from one perspective, this was the "darkest Fourth of July which has dawned upon us since the commencement of our national existence," but from another perspective, this Fourth was the "brightest." Greeley detailed the destruction of war: the

trouble has come—in blood, in debt, in public apprehension, in sickening anxiety. . . . Peace has gone. We have lost the serenity of becoming a great people; we have lost under the inevitable demoralization of War, a moiety of our virtues; the deep foundations upon which substantial commercial credit should rest, have been shaken; our days have been embittered by multiplying fear, and our nights have been full of dreams which disturb our sleep; our homes have been made desolate, and the bones of our loved ones are bleaching far away from the altar and fires which were abandoned.

But still Greeley did not despair, for he saw that out of the cauldron of war idealism would conquer materialistic aspirations; slavery would end:

This is the sunrise of the nation's moral prosperity. We may be materially poor, but we shall be rich in fidelity to the great ideas which underlie the welfare of the nation. We may be distracted by doubts of policy, but no longer by doubts of principle . . . our recognition of Human Equality [will] no longer [be] a dubious or dishonest experiment.[25]

The modern newspaper reader could envy his nineteenth-century counterpart, who had the chance to read Greeley's editorials regularly on issues of supreme national moment. One of the great regrets, when Greeley died, was the loss of that special insight, sharp wit, biting sarcasm, and elevating phrase so characteristic of Greeley's editorial prose.

CHAPTER 3

The Patron

A S A promoter, publisher, and employer of American authors,
Horace Greeley contributed vitally to the creation of a distinctive American literature. To Greeley, American democratic
nationalism depended on an independent intellectual heritage nurtured by talented American writers. Because of his own struggles to
find outlets as an editor and writer, Greeley understood the special
commercial and political pressures placed upon American authors.
That was why he sought to expand opportunities for potential writers:
he was always willing to instruct them in the publishing game. As a
man of practical bent as well as of artistic ambitions, Greeley realized
that some writers needed prodding and encouragement. While he
certainly did not appreciate the merits of all, he possessed enough
openness of spirit to seek space for those with whom he might
disagree. Hence the *Tribune* became a forum for informed, public
debate over the future of American letters. In some ways, one of
Greeley's most fundamental commitments was to the literary arts.

Not only did Greeley contribute directly to American letters
through his own special literary works, but he also spent much
energy sponsoring the careers of some of America's finest writers in
many ways, from editorial salutes to their books, to direct employment, to service as a literary agent. A brief catalog of those whom he
patronized suggests that Greeley was the William Dean Howells of
his generation: among those he helped were Edgar Allan Poe, Walt
Whitman, Mark Twain, and two of the most significant, Henry David
Thoreau and Margaret Fuller. Furthermore, any examination of
Greeley's correspondence with some of these individuals reveals that
Greeley's patronage benefited his own growth as "Man Thinking," in
Ralph Waldo Emerson's phrase, since clearly his practical dealings
with such luminaries influenced his own style.

Indeed, Greeley's ability as a writer reflected not only his cultivation of a distinctive personal style, but also his commitment to literature as a necessary, refreshing human activity. Greeley's devotion to letters was shaped in youth. As a young man, he said, he had always read prodigiously, and as a young editor, he had at first shunned politics and sponsored the *New-Yorker*, which was committed to the literary arts. Greeley's temperament embodied the classic tension between the man of action and the man of ideas. Like some Transcendentalists, he wished to transform this traditional dualism into the monistic Emersonian ideal of the American Scholar. Greeley's belief in letters lent force to his conviction that men of power would all be inherently corrupt without the curtailing currents of introspection experienced in the literary enterprise. For Greeley wanted to enlarge the possibilities of freedom by sponsoring as many potential talents as possible.

In his essay, "Literature as A Vocation," Greeley cautioned ambitious young writers against catering to their reading public for commercial success; he advised them to accept the risks of initial penury in order to establish an intellectual independence and to create works of high quality for future generations: "the peril of the Literary vocation is compliance,—the sacrifice of the eternal verity to the temporary necessity. To write to-day for to-day's bread involves the necessity of writing what today will appreciate, accept and buy . . . this tendency may be resisted, baffled, overborne, but it can never cease to be a reality." He termed Literature a "noble calling" and regarded talented young writers and editors as educators. Greeley saw literature as a form of public art, not a confessional of private emotions. Said Greeley, "if you are sure that your impulse is not personal nor sinister, but a desire to serve and ennoble your Race, . . . then all pray you not to believe that the world is too wise to need further enlightenment."[1]

I *Henry David Thoreau*

Greeley encouraged writers to have discipline, patience, and a social conscience. This was why an author exhibiting such qualities as Henry David Thoreau appealed to him, and why he would willingly support such writers. Out of his private experience, Thoreau spoke with public voice and with considerable conviction and daring. While Greeley's literary standards would probably not respond to the psychic impulses of much of twentieth-century literature, those same standards helped give the twentieth century one of the nineteenth century's immortal books, *Walden*.

As Walter Harding in *The Days of Thoreau* has stressed, Greeley
was instrumental in fostering Thoreau's publishing career. Having
met the promising writer in 1842 when he addressed the Concord
Lyceum at Thoreau's invitation, Greeley proved a ready friend and
consultant when the young Transcendentalist first visited New York
City in 1843. The two men liked each other immediately. Writing to
his sister Sophia in 1843, Thoreau paid tribute to Greeley as one "who
is cheerfully in earnest at his office of all work—a hearty New Hampshire boy as one would wish to meet—and says, 'Now be
neighborly.'" Greeley and Thoreau would correspond periodically
over the years; in the 1850's Thoreau visited Greeley's Chappaqua
farm and considered briefly an offer to tutor Greeley's children there.
In his journal, Thoreau recalled a visit to the opera with Greeley in
late 1854: "Greeley carried me to the new opera-house, where I heard
Grisi and her troupe. . . . Greeley appeared to know and be known
by everybody; was admitted free to the opera, and we were led by a
page to various parts of the house at different times."[2]

Six years Thoreau's elder, Greeley served Thoreau through advice
on publishing outlets, some positive accounts in the paper, an occasional role as literary agent. He obtained a publisher in *Graham's
Magazine* for Thoreau's "Thomas Carlyle and His Works" in 1846, and
he published portions of a private letter in which Thoreau thanked
Greeley for collecting a delayed payment of fifty dollars for the
article, an act which so impressed Thoreau that he inserted some
portions of the letter into the introductory passage of *Walden*, a work
which Greeley enthusiastically trumpeted when it was published in
1854. In the printed version of the letter, Thoreau stated that for "the
last five years, I have supported myself solely by the labor of my
hands. . . . For more than two years past, I have lived alone in the
woods, in a good plastered and shingled house of my own building."
In the final draft of *Walden*, Thoreau illustrated how he could shape
the rambling discourse of his letter into the disciplined, elegant
prose of his introduction: "When I wrote the following pages, or
rather the bulk of them, I lived alone, in the woods, a mile from any
neighbor, in a house which I had built myself, on the shore of Walden
Pond, in Concord, Massachusetts, and earned my living by the labor
of my hands only. I lived there two years and two months. At present I
am a sojourner in civilized life again."[3]

In a typically moral posture, Greeley in his commentary on
Thoreau's letter used the theme of self-sufficiency to scold other
young authors. Without identifying him by name, Greeley saluted

Thoreau as a "literary youth—a thorough classical scholar, true poet
. . . [who] never sought to make a livelihood by his writing."[4]

Greeley found in Thoreau a kindred spirit. Thoreau's respect for
the natural environment, his opposition to slavery, his independence, his Yankee heritage appealed to Greeley. Furthermore, he
appreciated Thoreau's willingness to shun commercial success in
favor of literary quality. Thoreau's praiseworthy account of Carlyle
corresponded with Greeley's view; in an 1846 letter to Thoreau,
Greeley said,

But I know you have written a good thing about Carlyle,—too solidly good, I
fear, to be profitable to yourself, or attractive to publishers. Did'st thou ever,
O my friend! ponder on the significance and cogency of the assurance, Ye
cannot serve God and Mammon; as applicable to literature,—applicable,
indeed, to all things whatsoever? God grant us grace to endeavor to serve
Him rather than Mammon,—that ought to suffice us. In my poor judgement,
if anything is calculated to make a scoundrel of an honest man, writing to sell
is that very particular thing.[5]

Clearly, Thoreau represented for Greeley what he had termed in
"Literature as a Vocation" as an aspiring writer who was daring
enough to risk current profit for future appreciation.

II *Margaret Fuller*

One of the most intriguing episodes of Greeley's literary life was
the close personal and professional relationship he developed with
Margaret Fuller. According to biographer Arthur W. Brown, Margaret Fuller first came to Greeley's notice through his reading her
Summer on the Lakes, for which he had high regard. However, Mary
Greeley was initially more intrigued with the famous lady Transcendentalist than was Horace; she had participated in some of
Fuller's "conversations" while on visits to Boston and had admired
Fuller's independent stance. In 1844, Greeley offered Fuller the
position of literary critic of the *Tribune*, the first such post ever
offered a woman in America.

At Mary's urging, Margaret moved into their Turtle Bay home and
there entertained several ladies with elevated dialogue about wom-
en's rights. Her work at the *Tribune* offices was equally impressive.
According to William Harlan Hale, Greeley helped shape Fuller's
style by trimming away needless flourishes and stressing a functional

writing process much like his own. Under his tutelage, Fuller produced some of her best passages and emerged as a champion of noted
American writers. For instance, her review of the *Narrative of Frederick Douglass* was incisive and appreciative: "Considered merely
as a narrative, we have never read one more simple, true, coherent,
and warm with genuine feeling. It is an excellent piece of writing, and
on that score to be prized as a specimen of the powers of the Black
Race, which providence persists in disputing."[6]

In his *Recollections*, Greeley saluted her as the "best instructed
woman in America." He called her *Woman in the Nineteenth Century*
"the ablest, bravest, broadest, assertion yet made of what are termed
Woman's Rights." He said that in her conversations "women who had
known her but a day revealed to her the most jealously guarded
secrets of their lives, seeking her sympathy and counsel thereon, and
were themselves annoyed at having done so when the magnetism of
her presence was withdrawn."[7]

Fuller was equally charmed by Greeley. In a letter to Eugene
Fuller, she said, "Mr. Greeley I like, nay more, love. He is, in his
habits, a—plebeian; in his heart, a noble man. His abilities, in his
own way, are great. He believes in mine to a surprising extent. We
are true friends."[8] Fuller rewarded Greeley's trust with a series of
reviews written from December 7, 1844, to August 1, 1846. In these
accounts, she critiqued works of such luminaries as Edgar Allan Poe,
Nathaniel Hawthorne, Herman Melville, James Russell Lowell,
Frederick Douglass, Charles Dickens, Robert Browning, Brockden
Brown, Henry Wadsworth Longfellow, Ralph Waldo Emerson, and
Thomas Carlyle.

With Greeley, Fuller shared a social conscience, a concern for the
impoverished in urban life. She was deeply affected by poverty she
saw in her visits to prisons like the Tombs in New York City. As
Greeley stated in his *Recollections:*

No project of moral or social reform ever failed to command her generous,
cheering benediction, even when she could not share the sanguine hopes of
its authors: she trusted that these might somehow benefit the objects of their
self-sacrifice, and felt confident that they must, at all events, be blest in their
own moral natures. I doubt that our various benevolent and reformatory
associations had ever before, or have ever since, received such wise, dis-
criminating commendation to the favor of the rich, as they did from her pen
during her connection with the *Tribune*.[9]

As he recalled many years later, Fuller's death in 1850 by shipwreck off the coast of New Jersey, when she was returning with her family after adventures in Italy, struck him with profound grief.

III *The "Cooperage" of the* Tribune

Greeley, with his typical irascibility, could and did offend some American writers. One of the most unfortunate and yet humorous episodes involved his clash with James Fenimore Cooper. In 1841, Cooper had sued Greeley's political ally Thurlow Weed for libel against *Home as Found* and had won a $400 verdict. As Glyndon Van Deusen reports, when Greeley printed Weed's rebuking statement against Cooper, he in turn sued the *Tribune* for $3,000, a case which resulted in a nominal triumph for Cooper at the cost of almost $300 for Greeley.[10]

During the judicial proceedings in 1842, Greeley mocked Cooper's action by dubbing his efforts as the "Cooperage" of the *Tribune*, but the ire of the famous creator of the Leatherstocking Tales was not assuaged. Beyond the important implications of what such libel suits meant for the constitutional right of a free press, Greeley's contest with Cooper indicated his anathema to the conservative posture of a man who could write *The American Democrat*, which was filled with strictures on the principle of social equality. Yet, in some respects, the disagreement between the two men was unfortunate, since both shared the commitment to the possibilities of the American experiment.

IV *Utopian Visions*

Other writers whose principles Greeley heartily endorsed were Utopian thinkers like Charles Fourier and Albert Brisbane, whose *Social Destiny of Man* and *Association* Greeley sponsored in the early 1840s. Greeley's interest in Utopian communities was stimulated by his personal awareness of rural and urban poverty and by his faith in the capacity of human beings to remake society. Accordingly, as Glyndon Van Deusen notes, Greeley's push for Association led him to include a Brisbane column from 1842 to 1843 at the very inception of the *Tribune*.

According to Alice Felt Tyler, Greeley and Brisbane showed their greatest interest in the famous Brook Farm, the Sylvania Phalanx of northern Pennsylvania, and the North American Phalanx, situated close to Red Bank, New Jersey. Greeley served as treasurer for the Sylvania experiment and invested thousands of dollars in it. All ended in failure.[11]

V *Portents for American Literature*

In his sponsorship of literary minds, Greeley displayed his deep conviction that in order for Americans to achieve cultural independence, opportunities for struggling and vital creative spirits must be broadened. Because of his own youthful trials, Greeley well understood the severe limitations American society still placed on writers; this was a time when writers could depend on no ready patronage from academic positions, associate editorships, or publishing positions. One of the few channels available was the field of journalism; hence Greeley the editor sought to use every means of journalistic power to employ literary artists, to provide them with a steady income, to match creative writers with creative readers. He crusaded for an international copyright law to protect American works from being pirated abroad. If, at times, Greeley faltered in his reach for political power or misused what political capital he had amassed, he used his editorial power wisely. In his role as editor, Greeley was a most effective broker for young writers; hence some might observe that if, as Reinhold Niebuhr has said, there is power for justice, Greeley's manipulations on behalf of creative American artists marked one of his finest achievements.

But, more than this, Greeley's patronage illustrated his capacity to read with discernment and to grow from his interaction with other stimulating spirits. That was why his *Tribune* offices remained not only a citadel for his readers' enlightenment, but also for his own. For, by conversing with such independent souls as Henry David Thoreau and Margaret Fuller, Greeley deepened his range of knowledge, and the power of his style matured. Greeley as patron was a supreme educator to those he supported; he advised them on practical affairs, and in so doing, he enhanced the quality of his own and of American intellectual life.

CHAPTER 4

The Reformer

A S AN essayist, Horace Greeley could be disappointing. In its worst form, his prose was bombastic, wordy, convoluted, even dull. Yet Greeley's published essays had high literary moments. While not sustaining the brilliance of Ralph Waldo Emerson's best efforts, Greeley, in such works as *Hints Toward Reforms* (1850), could achieve passages of unique insight and eloquence. One should recall that most of Greeley's essays were like Emerson's, oratorical in style because they were first delivered as lectures. Today, they read better than they must have originally sounded, for as Greeley admitted, "I am . . . not a fluent nor effective speaker." As James Parton noted in describing one of Greeley's lectures, his "attire is in a condition of the most hopeless, and, . . . elaborate disorder. . . . The voice of the speaker is high-pitched, small, soft . . . Horace Greeley is . . . no orator."[1]

I *Emancipation of Labor*

The *Hints Toward Reforms* remains an impressive collection because it presents Greeley in his most persuasive tone as a reformer. It is an anthology of talks given in the 1840s on a wide variety of subjects, ranging from labor to education to temperance to transcendentalism to social utopianism.

Of course, in the 1840's Greeley was deeply immersed in the intellectual currents of reform, what historian Alice Felt Tyler has called *Freedom's Ferment*. Among those who deeply influenced Greeley was Albert Brisbane, whose *Social Destiny of Man* (1840) and *Association* (1843) were important contributions to Utopian literature. Here was a Greeley mature and confident in thought after the personal struggles of the 1830s and deeply committed to a wide variety of causes in a growing industrial society. Later, like other reformers, he would be devoting most of his public energies to ending slavery. Furthermore, this volume contained one of the most

remarkable pieces he ever wrote, his tribute to the mind and character of the French socialist Charles Fourier.

Essential to Greeley's thought was the principle of progress in the
conditions of the human environment as well as in the human character itself. Counseled by his Puritan heritage, Greeley perceived the
flaws in human conduct, the imperfections of the human spirit, the
manipulative tactics of the powerful, the reality of human evil. Yet, he
was a representative man of his age, in the best sense of Emerson's
phrase, in that he refused to relinquish his faith, nurtured in romanti-
cism, that human beings could be much more creative, sensitive,
contributing individuals if given a wider forum. He stressed the
principle of amelioration of the human condition and the possibility
that a greater degree of secular happiness could be achieved. As he
said in "Emancipation of Labor," "Let us give human nature a fair
trial, and see if it utterly lacks sense as well as any glimmering of
virtue, before we pronounce it as a hopeless failure to be managed
only with the straight-jacket and the halter."[2]

Central to this faith, Parton said, was the need for emancipation
not just for slaves but for all Americans. In a letter to an antislavery
group in 1845, Greeley said that he opposed slavery in all its forms,
not just more distant forms of oppression in the South, but that of the
laboring masses and the free blacks of the North. Greeley stated that,
"I understand by Slavery, that condition in which one human being
exists mainly as a convenience for other human beings." Furthermore, Greeley argued that unless Northerners granted free blacks
full opportunities, they would be subject to Southern critiques that
their treatment of "free" blacks was worse than slavery, as it represented a wide deviation between promise and reality.[3]

To Greeley, the root of slavery was the question of unearned
privilege, hence the unjustified division of human beings into classes.
Greeley elaborated that slavery consisted of six elements: enforced
obedience and servitude to other human beings, membership in an
inferior class, land tenancy rather than ownership, underemploy-
ment in terms of power and pay, acceptance of a leisurely and idle
wealthy class, and the assumption that one class was to be served and
not obligated to return the service to society.

Greeley, in a letter in 1850, summarized what he termed the
"progressive ideas of our time" as "Land Reform, Labor Reform, Law
Reform, Protection to Labor, Cheap Postage." Here Greeley
stressed natural rights established by the American Revolution,
rights to life, liberty, property, and the pursuit of happiness. Under

his reforms, Greeley asked for equitable distribution of land owner-ship as long as there was any which had no private owner, a "legal definition and limitation of a day's work," a "simplification of . . . legal processes . . . so as to render justice cheap, prompt and easily accessible to all," the principle of a high tariff so that American labor would not be subject to "a shameful competition with the famished labor of Europe," an open mailing system so that all could enjoy "the benefit of the inexpensive diffusion of Truth and Thought."[4]

Greeley linked economic realities with Enlightenment idealism. He understood that central to a free and peaceful exchange of ideas was the legal guarantee of economic stability to each individual. Hence, in order for men to converse in open and worthwhile dialogues, their postage must be cheap, their justice accessible to all, land and jobs fully available, daily leisure time guaranteed. Before there could be a true intellectual democracy there must be economic democracy. As he stated in a letter in 1847, "The basis of True Democracy . . . is to be *Land Reform*, not alone as applied to the Public Lands, but to *all* Lands. With this goes *Labor Reforms*." And in another letter in 1852, Greeley articulated his concern with the foundations of an emerging American culture.

To my mind, the *Bread* problem lies at the base of all the desirable forms which our age meditates. Not that Bread is intrinsically more important to man than temperance, intelligence, morality and religion, but that it is essential to just appreciation and healthful acquisition of all these. Vainly do we preach the blessings of Temperance to human beings cradled in hunger and suffering . . . the agonies of famine, idly do we commend Intellectual Culture to those whose minds are daily rocked [with] the dark problem "How shall we procure food for the morrow?" Morality, Religion are but words to him who fishes in gutters for the means of sustaining life and crouches behind barrels in the street for shelter from the cutting blasts of a winter's night.[5]

The most poignant passages in this series of lectures were those where Greeley became the voice of the poor. These statements, less analytical than other sections, held special impact because of the richness of descriptive detail. Influenced by his reading of Thomas Carlyle, Greeley argued that many Americans expected too much of their poor in an industrial society if they thought that special aids were not often needed to better their lot. He understood the unique social conditions which a life of poverty entailed; a celebration of unique cases of upward mobility were not sufficient to inspire an end of poverty. But he also refused to accept the maxim "the poor, ye shall always have with you." Said Greeley,

no more can just and luminous ideas of his own nature, relations, duties, and destinies be expected often to irradicate the mind of one doomed to a life of object drudgery, penury, and privation. Show me a community, a class, a calling, wherever poverty, discomfort, and excessive, unrewarded toil have come to be regarded as an inexable destiny, and I will tell you that there the laws of God and Man are sullenly defied or stupidly disregarded.[6]

In the essay "The Organization of Labor," Greeley criticized indifferent and oblivious attitudes of wealthy, educated Americans toward the poor. Furthermore, Greeley castigated the use of Christian themes to sustain a culture of poverty. Addressing his "conservative" friends, Greeley contended that such people would admit the existence of American penury but will

contend that it is divinely ordained. . . . He seeks not to deny that whole neighborhoods are famishing—but what of it? Did not Christ say, "Thy poor ye have always with you?" . . . Starvation and wretchedness are by Heavenly appointment—sent to discipline partly, well-to-do Christians in the exercise of Charity. Thus the poor famish, but that only proves the extent of human perversity, the desperate viciousness and depravity of the lower class, or the fierceness of the Divine wrath against Sin, and Society stands acquitted of injustice or even improvidence. When some poor peasant, living with his pigs and children in a mud-hovel unfit for the habitation of brutes, driven to despair by the impossibility of subsisting his family and paying some dollars' rent for a scant half acre of soil, falls into habits of intemperance, and is ejected for non-payment of rent, *his* fault is exaggerated and his calamity deemed a righteous retribution; while his landlord, who idly enjoys and uselessly expends an income of $50,000 or more, racked from just such half-acres and hovels, walks the earth an honored, smiling, self-satisfied Christian gentleman, the pride of the country and the idol of those he honors with his intimacy; and when at a ripe age he is gathered to his fathers, florid sermons are preached in commendation of his exemplary life and in glorification of the munificent charity which he gave back to plundered Poverty a hundredth part of what he took from it.

Greeley also counseled against the habit of avoiding the issue of poverty at home by seeking its elimination in Ireland, Europe, or other places abroad: "not in Ireland only, nor in Europe, nor in the Old World, are there grievous Social wrongs to redress, but here and everywhere."[7]

In a pre-Darwinian age, Greeley criticized what men like William Graham Sumner would later uphold: that social classes owed nothing to each other. Said Greeley, man

deals hardly with his brother—the rich with the poor, the strong with the weak, the landed with the landless. The base of our Social Edifice is not Justice but Power—the right of the strongest to use his strength, not to upraise but to depress his brother, if he can seemingly profit thereby. . . . Let bread become scarce, and what Christian merchant, what affluent farmer hesitates to advance the price of grain, though the wail of the famished is ringing in his ears?[8]

Greeley introduced a Whitmanesque gallery of portraits of social injustice: the young craftsman unable to find employment despite his proven skills; the poor laborer who could not support his family; the poor youth of "Liberal Education" who could not find a job in a society which demands technical skills; the seasonal day-laborer who was denied a position in the winter; the poor widow; the prostitute. In his call for awareness of those situations from affluent Americans, Greeley resembled a Michael Harrington of the twentieth century.

One remedy Greeley proposed was the introduction of what he termed "industrial education," a realistic program designed to train poor youngsters in skills needed in modern, industrial states. In this sense, he anticipated job training programs of the twentieth century. To Greeley, satisfactory employment was a right for all Americans, not just a *privilege*.

II *Charles Fourier*

In Emerson's terms, Greeley stressed the role of the imaginative as well as the manipulative mind. Without vision, men and women would never be freed from the provincial concerns of daily life. Said Greeley, "if we are educated slaves or enslavers, we shall rarely and with difficulty outgrow our early lessons, and become true men and women. . . . Men are becoming slowly but sensibly averse to whatever creates barriers between them and cuts them into fragments and particles."[9]

One solution Greeley proposed for some Americans came from the influence of Charles Fourier on his thought, a version of social utopianism which he termed Association. Utopian communities were to be offered as options to Americans, not as a system which would become the national order. Greeley's description of the ideal Fourierst community was a more flexible one than stricter social planners of his day imagined. His social utopia was one means to an end: the eradication of poverty and the liberation of each, independent spirit.

Greeley's reforming zeal, as biographer Glyndon van Deusen has stated, did have limitations. His belief in Association with its basis in the romantic goal of universal brotherhood was undefined, vague, and somewhat naive. In his essay, "Reforms and Reformers," Greeley defined a reformer as a "transformer," an individual who was the moderator between the extremes of radicalism and conservatism.[10] This vision of the reformer was mild compared to other crusaders of his day: Greeley was no revolutionary; he wanted to make the system more just, not to change it. Some of his specific reforms were narrow in conception. In labor reform, he opposed the strike, and for child labor, he simply said that those under eighteen should work no more than ten hours a day. At first he tended to confuse the issue of slavery by equating it, as did some Southern defenders, with Northern wage slavery. Not until much later did he seem willing to answer power for injustice with power for justice, as Reinhold Niebuhr would say.

Part of the problem with Greeley's moderate prescriptions for societal problems, which he understood well, lay in his own belief in the ultimate rationality of men. He hated violence. He believed that if individuals could only open their minds, as he did, and see problems from a national, rather than a provincial perspective, solutions would come. The Puritan in Greeley recognized the darkness and irrational impulse in human beings. The Enlightened Greeley saw the possibilities of reason to control the darkness; the Transcendental Greeley succumbed to what Greeley called the "watchword of the Nineteenth Century . . . Brotherhood . . . the great discovery being made . . . by the children of men, is that of their community of origins, of interests, of aspirations." Greeley liked the image of Byronic heroes, because, while "misanthropic themselves, they yet inspire in us a deeper confidence and a loftier pride in humanity. We see their error, and avoid it if we choose; the trust they inspire in the yet unfathomed capacities of our nature endures."[11]

Greeley's faith in the unlimited potential of the human individual was a cause for frustration because of the shackles the human condition imposed on those possibilities. The theme of the visionary imprisoned in earthly vestments had special empathy for Greeley, who, while intensely involved in human activities, must have yearned for retreat. Nowhere did he better express the dichotomy between the actual and ideal than in his description of Fourier.

The world without and within such a man must present a strange and striking contrast. Around him poverty, neglect, derision—a settled hostility or a more humiliating indifference; within, the consciousness of mighty discoveries—of truths competent now and certain ultimately to transform and electrify mankind. Around him obstruction and want—perhaps hunger and cold; within, the deep conviction that he had discovered the means ordained of God for banishing want from the earth, by quadrupling production, renovating and beautifying the earth, until at last even the Polar Ices should be dissolved, and a joyous, exhilarating spring-time envelop our planet. The reclamation of deserts, of pestilential marshes, of wildernesses and snow-capped mountains, until all earth shall praise Heaven by comforting and blessing mankind—all these, and many more dizzying, are among the ultimate consequences of Social Reorganization, anticipated by Fourier.[12]

In his essays, Greeley served as the popular spokesperson for Americans teeming with demands for change in both life-styles and in the institutions which governed them. In his best efforts, he represented a fervent idealism he never lost.

CHAPTER 5

The Traveller

A T THE height of his influence and fame in 1859, Greeley decid-ed to take his own advice and go West. While he journeyed to mid-America several times earlier on lecture tours and for other matters—for instance, he had looked over mine holdings on Lake Superior in 1847—he had never seen the Rockies or the Pacific. Furthermore, Greeley used the opportunity to publicize the need for a transcontinental railroad and enhanced his own posture on the issue before the *Tribune* audience. There were political motivations for his trip as well: for example, he wanted to assess the situation in Kansas after that region's civil war over the slavery question. Most remark-able about the journey was the fine series of dispatches he sent to the *Tribune* office from May 15 to October 10; they were characterized by what Greeley recognized as having "freshness of observations."[1] His reports were later collected into a volume entitled *An Overland Journey*, which has remained one of the exciting travelogues of the nineteenth century.

I *Going West*

Glyndon Van Deusen has stated that Greeley was celebrated everywhere he went, and he effectively shared his excitement with his readers. But Greeley, an excellent reporter, did not allow his personal reception to interfere with the dispassionate stance of his statements, as he relayed skillful descriptions of everything he saw, from Kansas prairies to Indians and buffalo to a primitive Denver to Mormon country to the promised land of California. A. K. McClure stressed that Greeley believed "in the West, and in western people, and his early journey across the continent inspired him with even greater enthusiasm for western ideas and western progress."[2]

Beyond their historical and literary merit, Greeley's letters did credit to his character simply because he wrote them. As the editor of the distinguished *Weekly Tribune*, and as a political power, Greeley could have put aside "mere" reporting duties forever. But in this action as with others, Greeley once again displayed his antipathy toward any aristocratic perogatives.

The *Overland Journey* was filled with charming descriptions and anecdotes, some of them repeated later in Greeley's *Recollections*. For instance, Greeley commented on the immense numbers of buffalo he observed on the High Plains and on the senselessness of shooting them: "I would as soon think of shooting my neighbor's oxen as these great, clumsy, harmless creatures. If they were scarce, I might comprehend the idea of hunting them for sport; here, they are so abundant that you might as well hunt your neighbor's geese."[3]

His sketch of violent "Western" habits was marked by good humor and was reminiscent of the origins of villainous images in Western films. In his portrayal of the "old mountaineers" of Colorado, "a caste by themselves," he observed that there have been "during my two weeks' sojourn, more brawls, more fights, more pistol shots with criminal intent in this log city of one hundred and fifty dwellings . . . than in any community of no greater numbers in earth." He stated that they were "prone to deep drinking, soured in temper, always armed, bristling at a word, ready with the rifle, revolver or bowie knife." In the Denver House, Greeley recounted, the "visitors of [the] drinking and gambling room had a careless way, when drunk, of firing revolvers, sometimes at each other, at other times quite miscellaneously, which struck me as inconvenient for a quiet guest. . . . So I left."[4]

Toward Indians, Greeley displayed an ambiguous attitude typical of many white Americans as he shifted from paternalism to appreciation. Although he displayed his usual honesty in his observations, his bias did him little credit for modern sensibility. He accepted readily the conception of Indian culture as inferior because the Indian male was "not a worker, a producer." There was little sympathetic anthropological assessment of the Indian's unique life-styles. At one point, Greeley asserted that "Indians are children. Their rites . . . treaties, habitations, crafts . . . all belong to the very lowest and rudest ages of human existence." As a realist, Greeley did not accept romantic images of a "noble savage."

It needs but little familiarity with the actual, palpable aborigines to convince anyone that the poetic Indian—the Indian of Cooper and Longfellow—is only visible to the poet's eye. To the prosaic observer, the average Indian of the woods and prairies is a being who does little credit to human nature—a slave of appetite and sloth.[5]

Yet Greeley was not unjust: he did not dismiss hope for the American Indians, even if such optimism were nurtured by his own biases. While he typically relied on nineteenth-century ideals of Christianity and education for Indian salvation, he, somewhat surprisingly, looked toward Indian women to provide the foundation for a secure future, because they were hard workers and could influence Indian children in "civilized" ways.

II *Mormons and Popular Sovereignty*

The most unique feature of the reports was one of the first recorded interviews in the history of American journalism, the two-hour discussion with the Mormon leader, Brigham Young. In this famous interchange, Greeley's questions were eminently professional, restrained, and penetrating. Despite Greeley's disagreement with Mormon tenets, principally regarding the practice of polygomy, he let Young have his say and make his case: "If I hazard any criticisms on Mormonism generally, I reserve them for a separate letter, being determined to make this a fair and full exposé of the doctrine and policy, in the very words of its prophet."

Some Americans feared that "Mormonizing" the American West could corrupt it as much as the introduction of slavery. Hence Greeley's questions about slavery were pertinent. In answer to Greeley's queries, Young admitted that there were slaves held in the territory of Utah and that the territorial laws provided that if "slaves are brought here by those who owned them in the states, we do not favor their escape from the service of those owners." However, Young predicted that Utah would enter the Union as a free state, because slavery would "prove useless and unprofitable."[6]

In his subsequent report, Greeley recognized the enormous power the church held in Utah, a control which belied the American principle of separation of church and state. He raised the question of how national authorities should monitor this kind of power. Here Greeley made an intriguing attack on Stephen Douglas's notion of "popular sovereignty." As other critics had, Greeley argued that "popular sovereignty" in a territory was "a contradiction in terms,"[7] because it never resolved the question of what agency properly represented the popular will; while legislatures were elected by the people, they were also subjected to vetoes and checks by the governor, federal judges, and armed forces, appointed and directed by the federal government. When he argued that the people of a territory should decide the fate of slavery in their own region, Douglas never made fully clear how this was to be managed under territorial law; that was one reason, of course, for the Kansas war.

In his discussion of popular sovereignty in Utah, Greeley, with insight, made a distinction between the superficial national power and entrenched local power of the church: the agencies of Washington, "the federal judiciary, the federal executive, and the federal army, as now existing in Utah, are three transparent shams—three egregious forces"; they clearly did not represent the popular will. If any agencies represented popular sovereignty, they were the Utah legislature and the Utah courts. Indeed, the reality of popular sovereignty lay with the power of a person with no formal political office there, Brigham Young, who carried "the territory in his breeches' pocket without a shadow of opposition," because there was no "real power here but that of 'the church,' and he is practically the church." If popular sovereignty had any meaning in Utah, it would be to let Mormon officials govern the territory and to minimize federal intervention. Any other version of popular sovereignty would simply not work: "'popular sovereignty' in a territory, backed by a thousand sharp federal bayonets and a battery of flying artillery, is too monstrous a futility, too transparent a swindle, to be much upheld or tolerated."[8]

Here Greeley argued as Lincoln would with respect to slavery in the South. Lincoln felt that slavery should be localized in the region where it was legal and should not be allowed to spread. In this way, it would be checked; allow slavery into the territories, and it would be now "nationalized." While Greeley as an antislavery advocate certainly had misgivings about Lincoln's views, he employed the same reasoning about Mormonism. Rather than try to obliterate Mormon power, with its antidemocratic and polygamous posture, one should localize and check it by keeping Mormon territory as small as possible. In certain respects, Greeley used the same reasoning as James Madison had in *Federalist No. 10*: if one grants that the Mormons were a powerful faction, one should give them freedom and life rather than suppress them and then curtail them with other factions. Said Greeley, let "the Mormons have the territory to themselves—it is worth . . . little to others, but reduce its area."[9]

While Greeley's critique of popular sovereignty "notions" about Utah made sense, he did not leave a consistent record on the principle himself. Of course, despite his attack on popular sovereignty, his solution for Utah—leaving it to the Mormons—affirmed Douglas's principle that democracy guaranteed that the people of a territory should control their own life style. Apparently, Greeley agreed with Young that Utah would emerge as a free state. Also, when Greeley as a congressman in 1849 had addressed the House on the question of the reorganization of the New Mexican territory in 1849, he had argued for the separation of the New Mexican peoples from Texas because he feared the influx of Texan slavery into the new region. However, he conceded the principle of popular sovereignty when he asked that the "will of the people of New Mexico" should be considered: "Let them be the umpire. Let them determine whether [New Mexico] be an independent free Territory, or become part of the slaveholding State of Texas."[10] Also, when Greeley in late 1860 would argue that the country should consider letting the "erring" slave states depart rather than risk war, he invoked the principle of popular sovereignty with his argument that the question of secession should be decided by popular referenda in the Southern states. Of course, Greeley assumed that once the question of secession was calmly deliberated in the South, the majority would support the Union.

Yet Greeley had also firmly opposed Douglas's Kansas-Nebraska bill and condemned like attempts to put "popular sovereignty" in practice as a tactic to spread slavery. For this reason, he was one of the early organizers of the Republican party.

Greeley's dilemma over popular sovereignty was similar to the problem of other moderates like Douglas and Lincoln; how to oppose powerful institutions like slavery and the Mormon church, so alien to American principles of freedom of the individual, while simultaneously upholding the principle of American local democracy, how to coalesce local cultural distinctions like the Mormon practice of polygomy with national ideals. If Greeley's solutions to the dilemma were ambiguous in terms of Utah and the Southern states, his plight mirrored the views of many citizens.

Greeley also expressed concern for Mormon women, particularly after hearing Young's remarks about male supremacy. He noted their lack of power and their subservience and trusted that "the genius of the nineteenth century tends to a solution of the problem of woman's sphere and destiny radically different from this."[11]

Greeley presented a balanced judgment of the "Latter-Day Saints." While recognizing that there was generally little social interaction between "Gentiles" and Mormons, Greeley recorded his cordial reception. While some Mormons had undoubtedly killed

Gentile intruders on some occasions, most Mormons were "honest," "sincere," "just," "humane," hard working. As Greeley correctly observed, they, like his own Puritan ancestors, believed "they are God's peculiar and especial people, doing His work, upbuilding His kingdom." Those who appeared to "obstruct" this work were "God's enemy" and must be resisted.[12]

III *California and a National Railroad*

When Greeley reached his destination, California, he toured it widely and gave many speeches. He confidently forecast a beneficent future for a state of unexcelled physical beauty with an industrious population. For instance, with prescience, he said that San Francisco "could hardly fail to grow in population, trade, industry, and wealth." Its elements of greatness included a "magnificent harbor," an "equable climate," an "inexhaustible supply of the finest timber," the "richest mines," a "fertile . . . agricultural region," "a population rarely surpassed in intelligence, enterprise, and energy. . . . I bid her God speed."[13]

Central to Greeley's concern in his reports was the difficulty engendered by the patchwork quality of the national transportation system. Greeley appeared as the nationalist nurtured on Henry Clay's American system. In effect, his concluding plea for a transcontinental railroad came from his firm conviction that a strong technological network could sustain a compelling national community.

As he often did, Greeley first posited the opposing argument, that "a Pacific railroad is a humbug—the fantasy of demogogues and visionaries," and then with an impressive brief, full of an imposing catalog of facts and statistics, he decimated that initial impression. Actually, Greeley's recitation of his whole Western journey, with the difficulties encountered by traveling on stages across dusty roads, was a plea for a national railroad. Economically, California and the nation would benefit because the transportation of goods would pass through the nation rather than Panama; passengers would use the national railroad; and the mail could come more safely over a national route. In Greeley's view, the railroad would not only improve the material conditions of the citizens of the West; it would also improve the culture and hence the nation:

Men and brethren! let us resolve to have a railroad to the Pacific. . . . It will add more to the strength and wealth of our country than would the acquisi-

tion of a dozen Cubas. It will prove a bond of union not easily broken, and a
new spring to our national industry, prosperity and wealth. It will call new
manufactures into existence, and increase the demand for products of those
already existing. It will open new vistas to national and individual aspiration,
and crush out filibusterism by giving a new . . . direction to the public mind.
My long, fatiguing journey was undertaken in the hope that I might do
something toward the early construction of the Pacific railroad; and I trust
that it had not been made wholly in vain.[14]

CHAPTER 6

The Historian

TOWARD the end of his *Recollections* Greeley noted that at the opening of the Civil War he had not "thought of ever becoming [an] historian." But two events changed his mind: the issuance of the Emancipation Proclamation on January 1, 1863, and the subsequent "draft" riots in New York City in early July 1863. As Greeley stated,

not till that War was placed on its true basis of a struggle for liberation, and not conquest, by the President's successive Proclamations of Freedom, would I have consented to write its history. Not till I had confronted the Rebellion as a positive, desolating force, right here in New York, at the doors of earnest Republicans, in the hunting down and killing of defenceless, fleeing Blacks, in the burning of the Colored Orphan Asylum, and in the mobbing and firing of the Tribune office, could I have been moved to delineate its impulses, aims, progress, and impending catastrophe.[1]

After some hesitation, Greeley decided to accept a publisher's offer and begin the arduous task with his characteristic energy. Prior to the commencement of his daily editorial duties at the *Tribune* at noon, Greeley locked himself in a room at the "Bible House" and researched and wrote his history. With the help of a secretary, he visited nearby libraries for material and worked from one to three days on each chapter. The result was his first full-length book, composed as such rather than a compilation of previous shorter writings. Volume 1 of *The American Conflict* was issued in April 1864, and volume 2 followed in 1866.

I   The American Conflict: *Assessments*

Greeley's work, clearly the *magnum opus* of his writing career, has been the subject of much controversy. While the first volume sold well, Greeley's signing of Jefferson Davis's bail bond hindered the popularity of his second. While its treatment clearly mirrored much Unionist sentiment in the North, its Yankee bias would prove anathema in the South. Modern critics have differed widely. While, as recently as 1969, the bibliography in David Donald's and James G. Randall's *Civil War and Reconstruction* pronounced the book still "surprisingly useful" history,[2] William Hesseltine has said it was badly composed; and Thomas Pressly's major historiographical study, *Americans Interpret the Civil War,* mentioned the work only briefly as an example of Northern propaganda. Few modern critics have given the work a serious analysis.

Greeley himself recognized some of its limitations. In the preface to his first volume, he freely admitted his Northern bias when he stated that, in addition to Frank Moore's *Rebellion Record* and Orville O. Victor's *History of the Southern Rebellion,* he consulted the Southerner Edward Pollard's famous *Southern History* in order to avoid the errors and exaggerations of the Confederate viewpoint. In the preface to his second volume, which dealt largely with military affairs, Greeley acknowledged that, as a contemporary history, his book contained factual errors, but he promised to correct these in the future. In his *Recollections,* Greeley admitted that "an eminent antagonist of my political views has pronounced it 'the fairest one-sided book ever written.'"[3]

But Greeley also hoped it was "more than that." He confidently expected it would be consulted by historians long after his death, and he pronounced it "one of the clearest statements yet made" of the causes of the war. He thought his grandchildren would judge it "the most important and interesting feature of my work."[4]

Greeley saw his history as the culmination of a lifetime of labor in reform causes, and he wanted to link his personal agony over the slavery issue with the national struggle. The modern temperament can find much distasteful in these volumes. Greeley's subjective bias against the South, his "presentist" tendency to judge the past on his own terms rather than those of another era, and his rather disturbing comments about some so-called Negro propensities like laziness and ignorance would trouble modern sensibility. Yet the work represented massive research for its period, and as was characteristic of much of Greeley's writings, it was marked by a vigorous and powerful style in its character sketches, pieces of exposition, and narrative. It had insights which were still instructive over a century later, especially about the history of black Americans and the condition of slavery, and as document and history it deserves rereading. Certainly students of Civil War historiography should consult it carefully. And this is remarkable in that it was written by a man who was busily engaged in both national politics and the editorship of a great national newspaper.

Greeley's tomes derived their elemental power from the central thesis: the tragedy of the Civil War lay in the American nation's inability to rid itself of the cause of slavery at moments of opportunity, especially during the American Revolution. As he said in reference to the Missouri Compromise on slavery, "Had the majority then stood firm, they would have precluded the waste of thousands of millions of treasure and millions of blood." Greeley's main title, *The American Conflict*, underlined the theme of a national rather than sectional struggle. Slavery was the one corruptible element in the whole nation, not just the South, and it was the lack of moral consciousness in the entire nation which allowed slavery to fester and grow. In some ways, the absence of a powerful opposition to economic slavery in the North was as much a cause of the Civil War as the positive push for slavery in the South. Greeley stressed this point in a letter to Secretary of Treasury Salmon P. Chase in late December 1863: "We have embarked on the . . . experience of impelling a Pro-Slavery people to sustain an . . . Anti-Slavery War." As Greeley said in his *Recollections*, the "war was the natural and righteous consequence of the *American* people's general and guilty complicity in the crime of upholding and diffusing Human slavery." To Greeley, as to Abraham Lincoln in his second inaugural address, the war served as an example of how God determined "that every collision or compromise with evil must surely invoke a prompt and signal retribution." The war came because American democracy failed to uphold the central principle of its heritage, "the legal and National recognition of every man's right to himself."[5]

With such a universal theme, Greeley's work became a testimony to the struggle of a great people's attempt to match its ideals with practice, to end what Gunnar Myrdal would term many years later *The American Dilemma*. Because of Greeley's tendency to couple Transcendental optimism with Calvinistic skepticism, *The American Conflict* emerged as a telling portrait of the gradual corruptibility of American innocence with the evil of slavery. It was the balanced tale of failure and misery as much as that of success and progress. It was filled with the sadness of unneeded suffering; yet it celebrated the triumph of the kind of emancipation Greeley signaled in *Hints Toward Reforms*.

II *Origins of Slavery*

As Greeley stated in a letter written the same year as the first volume, Confederate victory would ensure the nationalization of slavery as an institution. Greeley predicted

not a separation but a reconstruction, by which the *whole* Country is to be surrendered to the Slave Power. It is very doubtful that conspicuous opponents of Slavery will be permitted to live *anywhere* in the United States. I have not for twenty years been at liberty to traverse unmolested, the Southern half of my own country. . . . A disunion triumph simply makes Slavery the arbiter of our *whole* country.[6]

Greeley's history was much more than the history of the war and its immediate causes; it was a history of the nation, an attitude study of white America's contradictory response to slavery and the black American. As Greeley wrote to a friend, Mrs. Whipple,

I have not usually believed that we should win, because I could not believe that we *deserved* to win. We are a Pro-Slavery people to-day. In the great city of Philadelphia, which gave Lincoln nearly 10,000 majority in '60, and again in '64, a black Union soldier is not allowed to ride in the street-cars; I tried to pilot through a respectable colored clergyman, but was obliged to give it up. By all ordinary rules, we ought to have been beaten in the fight and the more consistent and straightforward worshippers of Satan triumphant. Our great triumph is God's answer to the prayers of the Colored People; it is not *our* victory, and the result will show it. Whatever may now appear, the fruit of this great success will enure to the Blacks mainly.[7]

In *The American Conflict*, part of Greeley's subtitle, characteristic of the long descriptive and yet helpful titles of nineteenth-century books, before such became unfashionable in a more elliptic age, identified his purpose: "Intended to exhibit [the War's] moral and political phases, with the drift and progress of American Opinion respecting Human slavery from 1776 to [1865]." In a great editorial written prior to the war, Greeley succinctly summarized what would be the major principle of the war:

We have been regarded as engaged in trying a great experiment, involving not merely the future faith and welfare of this Western Continent, but the hopes and prospects of the whole human race. Is it possible for a Government to be permanently maintained without a standing army, and without either hereditary or self-appointed rulers? Is the democratic principle of equal rights, general suffrage, and government by a majority capable of being carried into practical operation, and that, too, over a large extent of country?[8]

Greeley's first volume opened with a description of the United States just after the American Revolution. While Greeley noted that the postwar period did not bring the "universal prosperity and happiness" which some hoped it would, and that the "illusion that the times that were are better than those that are, has probably pervaded all ages," he stressed that eighteenth-century life, with its social gatherings and slower pace, had its charm: "while his road to Mill and to meeting was longer and rougher than those we daily traversed, the Eighteenth Century man doubtless passed them unvexed by apprehensions of a snorting locomotive, at least as contented as we, and with small suspicion of his ill-fortune in having been born in the Eighteenth instead of the Nineteenth century." Yet by all measure of material progress, the nation by 1860 had fulfilled the vision of manifest destiny first established by the Founders; "The Great West of today owes its unequalled growth and progress, its population, productiveness, and wealth, primarily, to the framers of the Federation Constitution, by which its development was rendered possible."[9]

But Greeley coupled the vision of progress with the introduction of one element which marred the promise, human slavery: during the Revolution, said Greeley, "slavery was soon proven one chief source of weakness and of peril." Greeley introduced the heritage of darkness by at once scolding his forebears and pointing to the almost inevitable evolution of slavery on the American continent. After tracing the history of slavery in the early Spanish colonies, Greeley correctly asserted that the first black Americans were brought to the Anglo-American colony of Virginia several months before the Pilgrims landed in Plymouth. After the growth of slavery in the colonial period, Americans had a unique chance to abolish the institution in the cause of the American Revolution. Here, because of their commitment to the natural rights of each individual, the wisest revolutionaries envisioned the hypocrisy of trying to compromise on slavery:

The more discerning . . . patriots . . . confessed that their assertion of the rightful inseparability of Representation from Taxation necessarily affirmed the grander . . . right of each innocent, national being to the control and use of his own capacities and faculties, and the enjoyment of his own earning. The principles of civil and political liberty, so patiently evolved and thoroughly commended during the long controversy which preceded the appeal to arms, were reduced to axiom and became portions of the popular faith.[10]

Yet compromise, at times so necessary, prevailed, and Jeffersonian ideals were subverted. In a modernist tone, Greeley stressed how the Congress excised Thomas Jefferson's famous clause condemning the African slave trade from the Declaration because of opposition from the Southern colonies of Georgia and South Carolina.

Later, during the Confederation period, Congress also altered Jefferson's original ordinance for the organization of the Western territories by confining it to the Old Northwest. Here Jefferson's prohibition of the introduction of slavery in all the West was narrowly restricted to a Northern section: the chance for a national declaration of freedom in the West was lost. Said Greeley, "The Jefferson Ordinance, thus shorn of its strength, was like 'the play of Hamlet with the part of Hamlet omitted."[11] In a theme similar to Lincoln's, Greeley reiterated his belief that, if the West truly represented opportunity, it must be free. And in an insight which modern historians like Julian Boyd and Adrienne Koch have emphasized, Greeley underlined how Jefferson's original ordinance had provided a heritage of freedom which was sadly overturned. The principle of compromise took precedence over the issue of freedom in both the constitutional and all congressional debates since.

Greeley showed his own weakness as an historian by lapsing into preacherly tones drawn from his reform biases. The reasons for the forefathers' failure on this issue lay partially in their own moral weakness, he claimed. He stated, without much evidence, that "the moral condition of our people had sadly deteriorated through the course of the Revolution"; presumably patriots, under the strain of the cause, had turned to intemperance, profanity, licentiousness, infidelity, "sins" which Greeley had always condemned. Hence the people's resistance to the evils of slavery was weakened. Also, those who first introduced slavery to Anglo-America, the Virginian settlers, were "an unusually bad type," and their need for a forced labor system derived from the growth of another "Greeley" evil, tobacco, "that bewitching but poisonous narcotic." Even Greeley's own New England ancestors deserved condemnation: "The austere morality and democratic spirit of the Puritans ought to have kept their spirits clear from the strain of human bondage." Even the physical appearance of the early blacks was not without blame; Greeley described the early slaves as "uncouth and repulsive."[12]

In a more penetrating fashion, Greeley recognized the forefathers' dilemma and their acceptance of gradual emancipation, a process begun in Northern states. After the initial antipathy between Africans and their white masters had dissipated,

it was inevitable that kindly feelings should frequently be reciprocated between them, leading often to devotion on the one hand and emancipation on the other. It was not without reason that the founders of our Republic and the framers of our Constitution supposed they had provided for the gradual but certain disappearance of slavery, by limiting its area on the one hand, and providing for an early inhibition of the slave-trade on the other.[13]

Furthermore, Greeley stated that the founders, having rejected arbitrary power in the British king, saw its appearance in slavery and hoped for its dissolution:

But to plant slavery on virgin soil—to consecrate vast and yet vacant territories to its extension and perpetuation—to conquer and annex still further domains expressly to increase its security and enlarge its power—are guilty dreams which never troubled the repose of the great body of our Revolutionary sages. . . . Enlightened by their own experience as to the evils and dangers of arbitrary, despotic, irresponsible power, they were too upright and too logical to seek to fasten for all time on a helpless and inoffensive race chains far heavier and more galling than those they had just shaken off. Most of them held slaves, but held them under protest against the anomaly presented to the world by republican bondage, and in the confident hope that the day would soon dawn that would rid themselves of the curse and shame of human chattelhood.[14]

But with the introduction of the cotton gin and the spread of slavery westward, such hopes were blasted. Like many abolitionists, Greeley described how slavery undermined the American commitment to the familial unit. He stressed the "licentious and immoral connections between master and their bondwomen, so inseparable from the existence of slavery." Only in America would children of a parent, the master, be sent to the "auction-block" and be "[consigned] to eternal bondage among strangers." Greeley condemned slave-breeding and dreaded how American slaves had to endure ceaselessly the destruction of family ties:

The American [slave] is keenly aware that her [children] must share her own bitter and hopeless degradation. It was long ago observed that American Slavery, with its habitual and life-long separations of husband from wife, of parent from child, its exile of perhaps the larger portion of its victims from the humble but cherished homes of their childhood to the strange and repulsive swamps and forests of the far South-West, is harsher and viler than any other system of bondage on which the sun ever shone.[15]

As Greeley emphasized in his *Recollections*, two major events served to awaken both his private and the nation's conscience concerning the perpetuation of slavery; first, the murder of Elijah P. Lovejoy in 1837 and, second, the annexation of Texas in 1845 and the subsequent Mexican War in 1846. Clearly, the slave power attempted to subvert the principles of the American Enlightenment not just in the South, but in the North, in the nation and in the world. Greeley stated that "it was the purpose of the framers of the Constitution to render the inhabitants of all the states substantially and perpetually one people, living under a common Government, and known to the rest of mankind by a common national designation." Greeley emphasized in Lovejoy characteristics similar to his own: although a minister, Lovejoy spoke boldly against slavery, was a man of peace, and used the free press, in *The Observer*, to circulate his antislavery views. When he was forced to leave St. Louis because Missouri was a slave state, Lovejoy established himself in St. Charles, Illinois, only to be attacked and killed by a mob determined to silence expressions of antislavery in a "so-called" free state. Greeley stressed Lovejoy's moderation, his religious bearing, his decency, his love of American principles of free speech and press. Yet, "he was proscribed, hunted, persecuted, assaulted, plundered, and finally killed—not because he persisted in opposing slavery in the wrong place, or in a peculiarly objectionable manner, but because he would not desist from opposing it at all."[16]

Greeley saw tragic international implications in the annexation of Texas. No longer could America hide its "national cancer," slavery, behind the emblem of the American dream; now the lie to the American promise would be apparent to all. Greeley, somewhat ahistorically, interpreted the admission of Texas as just another power grab by slavocracy for extension of its influence:

But, up to this time, Slavery had sought and obtained the protection and championship of the Federal Government expressly as a domestic institution—as an important interest of a certain portion of the American people. In the Annexation of Texas, and in the reasons officially adduced therefore, it challenged the regard of mankind and defied the conscience of its own criticizers as a great national interest, to the protection of which all . . . our Government was inflexibly committed, and with whose fortunes those of our country were inextricably blended. For the first time, our Union stood before the Nation, not merely as an upholder but as a zealous, unscrupulous propagandist of Human Slavery.[17]

In narrating the immediate causes of conflict, Greeley effectively delineated the collapse of the American democratic process to confront the challenge of slavery. In this failure, America was denying its own national essence. While Greeley recognized that "political compromises . . . are a necessary incident of balanced governments," he felt that by the late 1840s and 1850s such balance was giving way to imperialistic ambitions of slaveholders. The Mexican War, the Fugitive Slave Act, popular sovereignty, the Dred Scott Case, the Kansas Civil War and its aftermath, John Brown's raid, the secessionist movement, all symbolized the triumph of power over principle, the denial of the possibility that blacks could be free citizens, a fact "refuted by the action of several of the Slave states themselves." Even in the South in late 1860, Greeley was convinced, the majority favored union over secession but through Southern devices of sectional power could not be heard. To Greeley, the push of the Southern slaveocracy attacked American democratic nationalism. As Greeley said, "The right of the people to modify the institution is one thing, and the right of a small faction or segment of a people to break up and destroy a Nation, is quite another." When Southern power lifted its hand against "our Nationality," the tragedy of civil war ensued: "And so we were plunged into the horrors of Civil War, the bloodiest struggle that America ever witnessed."[18]

III   *Emancipation*

To Greeley, only with the issuance of the Emancipation Proclamation and the suppression of the New York City rioters in 1863 did the moral conscience of the American democracy emerge supreme. In the second volume, published after the close of war, Greeley, while giving careful attention to the military events, did not neglect the home front. He wrote how Lincoln, at first hesitant, finally issued the Preliminary Proclamation of September 22 under the pressure of calls like Greeley's own in "The Prayer of Twenty Millions." Lincoln's gradual movement toward emancipation reflected the nation's: "From an early hour of the struggle, the public mind slowly and steadily gravitated toward the conclusion that the Rebellion was vulnerable only or mainly through Slavery."[19]

Partially, said Greeley, the war itself had changed white Americans' attitudes toward blacks. For instance, the "anti-negro prejudices" of white soldiers "quite commonly experienced a gradual change, under the discipline of service at the front, where they found every black their ready, active, zealous friend, and nearly every slaveholder or overseer their quiet but deadly, implacable foe." After Lincoln issued the "absolute Proclamation of Freedom" on January 1, 1863, he opened the way for the employment of black soldiers, a call issued in the document. The performance of the black military further strengthened the "transition in white attitudes." The resistance at first to arming blacks was blatant because it would undermine every vestige of class and caste in America; to Greeley, who had always stressed upward mobility, black soldiery was a necessary response to the need for emancipation of another dispossessed people. Many knew, said Greeley,

that a systematic arming of the Blacks in defence of the Union imposed obligations and involved consequences incompatible not merely with the perpetuation of Slavery, but with that of caste as well. Hence, the proclaimed repugnance in Congress, in the Press, and among the People, to owning the Blacks, was quite as acrid, pertinacious, and denunciatory as that which had been excited by the policy of Emancipation.

Greeley recognized the special contribution of black troops; he praised their "unquestioning obedience," "local knowledge," endurance, bravery; some black regiments were even superior to their white counterparts; "those Whites who fought . . . by their side will be the last to detract from the gratitude wherewith the Republic fitly honors all her sons who freely offered their lives for the salvation of their country."[20]

Yet, in describing how blacks helped change white attitudes, Greeley betrayed some disturbing views of his own, best termed a kind of benevolent paternalism similar to that expressed toward Indians in *An Overland Journey*. While calling for black freedom and citizenship, Greeley tended to deny black equality, an inconsistency representative of others of his liberal persuasion. He spoke of the blacks' "docility," their inferiority in "intelligence and tenacity"; "no wise General," he continued, "would have counted a corps of them equal, man for man, in a great, protracted battle, to a like number of *our* Whites. . . . To exalt them to the disparagement of *our* White soldiers would be as unwise as unjust."[21] Greeley's treatment showed that many antislavery advocates could also compromise their principles.

Despite his ambivalence about blacks as human beings, Greeley's most powerful passages in his history were reserved for his description of the draft riots. These represented the last attempt of Northern prejudice to halt the emancipation of blacks. Greeley had been a strong supporter of conscription, and he had courageously withstood the attempt of mobs, who opposed a draft for a war for black freedom, to disrupt his *Tribune* offices. Greeley said that the majority of Americans had resisted the antislavery cause of the war until the draft riots. After they were controlled, "public opinion had grown to the full stature of the Proclamation of Freedom, and had settled into a determination that Slavery must die and the Union survive." The mobs, many of them recent Irish immigrants, committed crimes "in an exhibition of human fiendishness which the Nineteenth Century has rarely parallelled." Greeley described the sacking of the Colored Orphan Asylum, the hanging of an innocent black man because of his color, the devastation of black women, the terror of a hunted black boy; the "most revolting feature of this carnival of crime and villanous madness," said Greeley, "was the uniform maltreatment to which the harmless, frightened Blacks were subjected."[22] The conviction of Greeley's prose did him much credit.

To Greeley, the draft riots represented the last nightmare of a national aberration, its fool's errand into the labyrinths of slavery and consequent prejudice. When the war ended, a new national dedication to compassion and uplifting of the dispossessed would be realized.

In his military accounts, undoubtedly relying on some of the superb narratives of military events in the reports of the *Daily Tribune*, Greeley devoted long and intricate passages to descriptions of tactics, strategy, and activities in the major battles of the war. Josiah Grinnell stated that Greeley's

fidelity as a historian of the war is proven by an incident. There was a wide and warm discussion as to the positions and behavior of a certain general in battle, and the issue. To gain the truth apart from officer and romancer, [Greeley] wished to hear the story of a private regular soldier on duty, then miles away from Washington. He asked me to accompany him, he being in disguise, with a pretext to call out the soldier, and guage the witness in the honesty of a simple, social narrative. To military men it was a secret, but all related to his history of the actors, the issue and strategy of war. He gained what he desired, only by a cold, muddy ride of six miles.[23]

While there were still some misconceptions in his reports, many of his judgments remained convincing. Greeley wanted to relay some of the cost and agony necessary to eliminate slavery. For instance, in describing Lincoln's appointment of General Ulysses Grant as "commander of the armies of the United States" in March 1864, Greeley stated that Grant, despite his limitations, was an apt commander because he understood the determination of the Confederate chieftains: no "love-taps, in his view, would ever persuade the Rebel chiefs to return to loyalty, so long as their military power should remain . . . unbroken; and he had no conception of any mode of breaking that power save by strong armies in bloody battles." Greeley acknowledged Confederate critics, who, like some modern doubters, had castigated Grant's methods in the Virginian campaign because he "aimed only to overpower and crush by brute force—by the employment of overwhelming numbers—and by a lavish expenditure of blood." Yet Greeley argued persuasively for the necessity of unpleasant means in a terrible war: other "campaigns were more brilliant; but none contributed more positively and eminently to break the power of the Confederates."[24]

As he said in his letter to Chase, "The country is fearfully weary of the cost, the sacrifices, the burdens inseparable from a great war."[25] As indicated by his Niagara venture, Greeley was willing to try negotiations, but he ultimately supported Grant's march because he saw it as the only way to peace.

Greeley's treatment of the war was balanced. While it had resulted in much unwanted, needless, and tragic suffering, it also created new possibilities for the American dream. It had forced America out of the grip of slavery, not just the slavery of a depressed economic, black peasantry, but the slavery of unenlightened white attitudes.

IV *Fruits of Victory*

After he completed *The American Conflict*, Greeley concisely summarized his central conclusions about the war. In an article entitled "The Fruits of the War," appearing in *The Galaxy* in 1867, he was one of the first to recognize that the Civil War was a modern war, modern because of the mobilization of huge national armies on both sides, the estimated cost of one million dead (military and nonmilitary), the large territory "traversed" with a "line of hostilities . . . at one time more than two thousand miles long," the destruction of at least five billion dollars worth of property. He counted over one hundred major battles; he stressed the long sieges of Charleston, Vicksburg, and Petersburg as among "the most persistent, sanguinary and memorable in modern history." He cataloged the weaponry made available with new techniques of industrial engineering: "Iron-clads, rams, rifled guns, steel projectiles, torpedoes." He emphasized the unconditional nature of the conflict: "never was struggle more determined, more vehement; never was triumph more absolute and complete." He pitched his thesis of triumph against those victors who insisted that the South must be further humiliated: "they yearn for human sacrifice beyond those which war itself exacted, and disdain a victory which is not ratified by the executioner," or otherwise, "the war has proved a failure."[26] As he would later in his presidential campaign, Greeley wished to push his nation toward the process of healing articulated so well in Lincoln's second inaugural address. Greeley remained closer to Lincoln's ideas than he might have cared to confess.

Greeley listed four permanent achievements of victory: the preservation of the Union; the abolition of slavery; the end of the threat of future civil war; the death of the supremacy of state sovereignty. Permanent "disunion" would have led to powerful and costly standing armies in both nations, hence inaugurating an era of uncontrolled military power.

To Greeley, the nation had directed its power toward noble ends: it freed itself from the perpetual curse of an institution which was destroying its people. The establishment of a supreme national authority as a result of the war had countered the corruption of the unchecked power of an evil labor system. All had suffered from that institution: slaves, masters, poor whites, the Southern region, the nation. Slaves would no longer be "scourged, pinioned, sold" without "prospect, . . . reward, . . . legal protection." Greeley, who despised divorce, stated that "even the sacred marriage bond might at any moment be shivered on the auctioneer's block." There was no clear reward system in slavery; everywhere was punishment. If slaves displayed "industrial capacity, . . . general efficiency, . . . trustworthiness," they were still denied; if they were "humble, dutiful, honest, diligent, pious," they still might merit the "whip." In an argument typical of abolitionists, Greeley stressed how whites were injured by slavery. With slaves serving them, the "slaveholders' children were not . . . trained to habits of industry and usefulness. They . . . could not degrade themselves . . . by any form of manual toil." Furthermore, even "poor whites" resented labor fit only for slaves. In short, slavery bred not a paradise, but a version of modern Hades, a land of "idlers" and few "workers."[27]

To Greeley, slavery denied all the American virtues: the value of hard work, energy, national commitment, economic progress, familial sanctity, democracy. Like critics of the imperial presidency in the twentieth century, Greeley felt slavery spawned a class of corrupt managers and manipulators who, entranced with power, would use any means to pursue their narrow and immoral purposes, at the expense of national ideals.

With emancipation, no more power arrangements would be determined by the Mason-Dixon line, by pitting North against South. Sectionalism would be dead. Emancipation would change corrupt attitudes and increase the productive power of the South. The power of a beneficent, not militant, federal government would be ascending: "It is not a 'reserved right' of any State to pronounce an act of Congress invalid. . . . Our political system has weak points; but nothing . . . so glaringly undemocratic, as a doctrine which would authorize one hundred thousand people to overrule and nullify the deliberate judgment of thirty millions." In a spirit which would predominate in his campaign of 1872, Greeley asked, "let us unitedly labor to restore the era of good feelings while we rebuild the waste places of our common country."[28]

V *Greeley and Lincoln*

Horace Greeley's reminiscences about Abraham Lincoln, expressed in the *American Conflict*, his autobiography, and an undelivered address in 1868, are fascinating to review because they offered a more balanced portrait than some of the exaggerated praise Lincoln received from other Northern political observers in the postbellum years. While Greeley, somewhat pettily, refused to recognize Lincoln's greatness, accepted by most today, he did render some fine insights into the Lincoln character. Yet he was not fully objective.

One reason for Greeley's lack of perspective came from his own uneasy relationship with the late president. While never intimates, the two men had known each other since they served as fellow congressmen in the second session of the thirtieth Congress in 1848–1849. Despite the difference of professions, both careers had striking similarities which William Harlan Hale stressed in the opening pages of his biography. They had both been born into poor, rural families, had been largely self-educated, had become successful through reliance on their own talents, and were superb craftsmen with the pen. Politically, they were extremely ambitious, but often failures in their tries at political office. Both men were Whigs and revered Henry Clay. Both would become instrumental in the formation of the Republican party. Yet they were frequently in opposition, particularly as Lincoln became nationally famous as a result of his debates in his senatorial contest against Stephen Douglas in 1858. In that campaign Greeley sided with Douglas, partially to keep the Democratic party divided. In 1860, Greeley, as a Republican delegate, had supported Edward Bates of Missouri at the national convention in Chicago and eventually came behind Lincoln only to keep William Seward, his old friend and now nemesis in New York State, from obtaining the presidential nomination. In 1864, Greeley had initially supported Salmon P. Chase for the nomination as a part of the Radical Republican movement, and he only supported Lincoln when the Chase "boomlet" collapsed with the fall of Atlanta in early September.

While praising Lincoln in his editorials after the assassination, Greeley often criticized the man who had the position of power which he himself sometimes desired. Once war began, Greeley both publically and privately said Lincoln was too slow in prosecuting the war and in committing himself to the goal of freedom as well as union. Yet paradoxically, Greeley felt Lincoln missed opportunities at achieving peace; in 1864, Lincoln wisely decided to let Greeley go to Niagara Falls to meet with supposed "peace" commissioners from the Confederacy, a scheme which failed partially because of the hypocritical nature of the commissioners. Here Lincoln could say that he had not stopped Greeley's mission, but he had extricated himself from taking responsibility for any results from such a misconceived adventure. Secretary of the Navy Gideon Welles confided in his famous diary that Lincoln, in reference to Greeley's correspondence on the Niagara mission, had declared in typical, anecdotal fashion that Greeley was

an old shoe,—good for nothing now, whatever he has been. "In early life, and with few mechanics and but little means in the West, we used," said he, "to make our shoes last a great while with much mending, and sometimes, when far gone, we found the leather so rotten the stitches would not hold. Greeley is so rotten that nothing can be done with him. He is not truthful; the stitches all tear out."[29]

The most famous point of public disagreement, of course, came with the issuance of Greeley's editorial, "The Prayer of Twenty Millions" of August 20, 1862, in which he called for a vigorous

emancipation policy under the authority of the second Confiscation
Act. Greeley had forewarned Lincoln of his stance both in his editorials and in an address entitled "The Nation," which he delivered at
the Smithsonian Institution with the president present in January
1862; there, to Lincoln's face, he had boldly attacked the administration's failure to develop an emancipation policy. Greeley argued
that the provisions of the new act were "designed to fight Slavery with
Liberty." Lincoln had ignored the implications of temporizing on the
slavery issue: the encouragement of disloyalty and of continued
Southern aggression. In this sense, only by coupling the goal of
freedom with that of Union could the Union be saved.

Here Greeley was not as radical as some abolitionists who were
calling for a document of immediate emancipation of all slaves.
Greeley seemed willing to allow loyal owners to keep slaves, at least
for the moment, and his chief criticism was that slaves would be
unwilling to support the Union effort unless the Confiscation Acts
were enforced.

Lincoln, who had signed the second Confiscation Act with great
reluctance, had already shown his cabinet a version of a preliminary
Emancipation Proclamation a month earlier. In his celebrated reply
to Greeley, Lincoln gave no hint of this. He committed himself to the
paramount object of saving the Union, whether all free or only
partially so. For the issue of slavery, despite Lincoln's personal wish
that it would disappear, was clearly subservient to the cause of
slavery.

I would save the Union. . . . If there be those who would not save the Union,
unless they could at the same time *save* slavery, I do not agree with them. If
there be those who would *not* save the Union unless they could at the same
time *destroy* slavery, I do not agree with them. . . . If I could save the Union
without freeing *any* slave, I would do it, and if I could save it by freeing all the
slaves I would do it, and if I could save it by freeing some and leaving others, I
would also do that.[30]

In his later comments on Lincoln, Greeley was perceptive because
there were similarities in Lincoln's growth to his own. Greeley noted
how Lincoln, an "heir of poverty and insignificance, obscure, un-
taught, buried throughout his childhood in the frontier forests," had
risen to become a "central figure of the Western Hemisphere."
Greeley stated how as a public man, a campaigner, Lincoln had
become responsive to democratic nuances:

He is day by day presenting facts and arguments and reading in the faces of his hearers their relative pertinence and effectiveness. If his statement of the case does not seem to produce conviction, he varies, fortifies, reinforces it, giving it . . . new shapes until he has hit upon that which seems to command the hearty, enthusiastic assent of . . . his hearers. And this becomes his model. Such was the school in which Abraham Lincoln trained himself to be the foremost convincer.

Greeley recognized the greatness of Lincoln's flexibility, his willingness to experiment, his humility. "Never did one so constantly and visibly grow under the discipline of incessant cares, anxieties and trials." Lincoln's life was characterized by "an unabated growth in mental and moral structure. Few have been more receptive, more sympathetic and . . . more plastic than he." He was a "genial, quiet, essentially peaceful man" who suffered greatly under the tragedy of the Civil War: "When I last saw him, a few weeks before his death, I was struck by his haggard, care-frought face, so different from the smug, gladsome countenance he first brought from Illinois."[31]

Greeley's view of Lincoln's presidency was mixed. He hailed the Emancipation Proclamation, which, despite its limitations, "recognized the right to destroy slavery whenever that step should be deemed necessary to the national salvation—nay, it affirmed the duty of destroying it in such contingency." He felt that the assassination was especially tragic because he knew of "few men better fitted to guide a nation's destinies in time of peace." He was "eminently fitted to soothe, to heal, and to reunite in lands of true, fraternal affection a people just lapsing into peace after years of distracting desolating internal strife."[32]

Yet Greeley felt Lincoln's leadership was inept in the Civil War. Until the first battle of Bull Run, Lincoln had not fully realized the severity of the rebellion he was confronting. While his firmness after that disaster was laudable, it also led him to mistakes. His refusal to recognize the Confederates as belligerents in any way closed off potential overtures of peace. Essentially, Greeley wanted Lincoln to pursue both war and peace more vigorously, but Greeley overlooked the difficulties in achieving two apparently contradictory goals. And he lacked a decided appreciation of Lincoln's subtleties, terming his "mental processes . . . slow, but sure."[33]

While Greeley claimed the country had produced greater men, he identified the Lincoln attributes which he admired: his commitments to democracy and the American nation. Greeley claimed that Lincoln, rather than the aristocratic Clay, deserved the epithet, "The Great Commoner": there "was no honest man who feared or dreaded to meet him, there was no virtuous society so rude that, had he casually dropped into it, he would have checked innocent hilarity or been felt as a damper on enjoyment." If Lincoln were a man for the people, Greeley also stressed that Lincoln would restore the national mission. Greeley recognized that ironically, had Lincoln ended the war early with a swift strike, slavery would have survived. In tones reminiscent of Lincoln's second inaugural address, which he admired, Greeley said, "The Republic needed to be passed through chastening, purifying fires of adversity and suffering; so these came and did their work and the verdure of a new national life springs . . . luxuriantly from their ashes."[34] Greeley was unusually candid when he recognized his own failure to support Lincoln's renomination.

In a Lincolnesque reference to William Shakespeare, Greeley said that

Hamlet's phrase, the "Divinity that shapes our ends," was quietly working out for us a larger and fuller deliverance than I had dared to hope for, leaving such short-sighted mortals as I no part but to wonder and adore . . . and gave us the one leader whose control secured not only the downfall of the rebellion but the external overthrow of Human Slavery, under the ploy of the Great Republic.[35]

In style and aspirations, Abraham Lincoln and Horace Greeley were closer than Greeley would admit.

CHAPTER 7

Autobiography

HORACE Greeley's *Recollections of a Busy Life* (1868) is another of his neglected works, yet it remains one of the outstanding autobiographies in American history. Full of charming perceptions, it invites comparison with the most famous American reminiscences, Benjamin Franklin's. For a man who knew so many among both the powerful and the dispossessed, and yet who was so strangely isolated, this book, particularly in the opening pages, provided some of the most revealing confessions Greeley ever wrote. He said in his "Apology," "I shall never put so much of *myself*, my experiences, notions, convictions, and modes of thought as [in] these *Recollections*." He termed the memoirs his "mental history."[1]

I *Major Ideas*

One of Greeley's major themes was how his formative years shaped forever his deepest principles: his beliefs in individualism, freedom, democracy, universal brotherhood; his commitments to hard work, education, nationalism, scientific farming, labor, reform, writing, and literature; his compassion for the poor and the slave; his balance between conservatism and liberalism; his preference for community and consensus over needless competition. Appearing initially as a series of articles for the *New York Ledger* and later revised, the *Recollections* provided a fascinating record of how this most representative of nineteenth-century men was deeply influenced by the intellectual currents of his era. In the book, Greeley saluted three of the shaping heritages on his life: Puritan Calvinism; the American Enlightenment; Transcendentalism. Out of these special traditions, Greeley introduced the most formalistic presentation of his personal philosophy. Certainly, Greeley had much to say to Americans in his book; the *Recollections* deserves a far wider reading than it now receives.

There was indirect evidence that Greeley may have patterned his book after Franklin's, but this remains speculative. In the *Recollections*, Greeley mentioned having read Franklin's *Autobiography* in the 1820s, and he was certainly conscious of how many called him the "Franklin" of his times. A few years later, John Greenleaf Whittier, at a celebrated dinner for Greeley in early 1872, designated him in this fashion, and in his biography, James Parton stated that, like "Franklin, he confines himself chiefly to the improvement of man's condition in material things, but he is a better man than Franklin; he is Franklin liberalized and enlightened; he is the Franklin of this generation. Like Franklin, he is more pious than religious, more humane than democrat."[2] While one may question Parton's superlatives, the link between Greeley and Franklin was clear.

Furthermore, in his lecture, "Self-Made Men," Greeley celebrated the majesty of Franklin's career, even when compared with George Washington's. Greeley admired in Franklin qualities which Greeley would reveal in himself: Franklin's commitment to American nationalism, his allegiance to American democracy, his self-mobility from a position of low status, his hard work, his public service, his writing ability, his role as tutor to youth. Greeley ranked Franklin above Washington "as the consummate . . . flowering of human nature under the skies of colonial America." He stressed that Franklin "toiled twenty arduous and precious years" to achieve the advantages which Washington had inherited at birth. Greeley liked Franklin's humility and his sense of alliance with the people even after he attained "power and world-wide fame." For Franklin was willing to write "a frank, ingenious confession of his youthful follies and sins for the instruction and admiration of others."[3]

The shape of Greeley's book paralleled Franklin's. Like Franklin, Greeley was born in New England of Calvinist heritage, but left to go to the Middle Atlantic region to seek prosperity. He was born in poverty and had little formal schooling but rose to prominence, fortune, and power. Greeley's arrival in New York City resembled Franklin's entry into Philadelphia. Like Franklin he began as an apprentice printer, later to become a famous editor and a celebrated writer. Both men were inventive and humanitarian; they performed enormous public services for their respective eras. And intellectually both paid tribute to their Calvinist heritage, while they also embraced a far more liberal theology, Deism for Franklin and Universalism in Greeley's case. Both books were most captivating in their recall of the early years of youth and became less personal after

Franklin and Greeley became more public figures. The Calvinist influence remained in their skepticism about human nature, although they both professed optimism for the future. Both works were periodically interrupted by brief sermons to the young; indeed, both authors confessed that the purpose of their books was to provide instruction for future generations.

Yet Greeley's book was also distinctive from Franklin's. Less humorous and more realistic, Greeley spoke more directly to his audience, while, as historian Russel Nye has stated, Franklin did a disservice to himself by creating an almost fictional character, a buffoon, a person, who, as the "I" of the narrative, was perpetually and yet hypocritically engaging. This made Franklin's work greater literature, but Greeley's better history. Of course, Greeley had the advantage over Franklin in that he found time to complete his work.

Unlike Franklin's, Greeley's work appeared contradictory. For a man who celebrated the phrase of Indiana editor Joseph Soule, "Go West, young man," Greeley as a youth found the West of his day in Ohio and beyond uninviting, and had to go East to New York City to find opportunity. While showing deep sympathy for the poor, he criticized "beggary." While confessing his love of the soil, he hated his own tough, rural background. While celebrating his Puritan ancestors, he rejected many of their tenets. While stressing openness of ideas and experiments in life-styles, he proved morally rigid about smoking, drinking, divorce. Denying he was an abolitionist, he became one of the most prominent antislavery advocates.

Yet a careful analysis of Greeley's thinking, as in the case of his editorials, revealed that the apparent contradictions often yielded to a basic consistency once the complexity of Greeley's ideas were given their due. Just as Greeley paradoxically would advocate full-scale war in 1861 to bring a quick peace after the bombardment of Fort Sumter, so he could eliminate other inconsistencies. He hated his youthful farming experience because it was unscientific and wasteful; he opposed Garrisonian abolitionists because they would not embrace political solutions, the only practical route for Greeley; he despised those poor who would not capitalize on opportunities as he had; he saw no need to be haunted by some meaningless tenets of Calvinism. Greeley in his thinking represented in many ways Emerson's man of understanding and reason. Transcendent in his vision of human possibility, he was nonetheless fully aware of human incapacities to fulfill that potential. The important thing was balance; while celebrating success, men and women should never forget failure. While having faith in progress, human beings must know that there will always be regress, always setbacks.

In many ways, Greeley's philosophy was Niebuhrian; never underestimate man's capacity for injustice but never overestimate his capacity for justice; appreciate the ideals of the children of light but do not overlook the wisdom of the children of darkness. Shattered often in life by the deaths of his children, Greeley significantly ended his book with a chapter entitled "My Dead," but in his last passage, Greeley, with characteristic equilibrium, stated,

My life has been busy and anxious, but not joyless. . . . I am grateful it has endured so long, and that it has abounded in opportunities for good not wholly unimproved, and in experience of the nobler as well as the basic impulses of human nature. I have been spared to see the end of giant wrongs, which I once deemed invincible in this century, and to note the silent upspringing and growth of principles and influences which I hail as destined to root out some of the most flagrant and pervading evils that yet remain.[4]

Greeley emerged as a more reflective person than the author of some earlier, more fiery editorials. While some of the old vitality was missing, the thinking was more poised.

II *Youth*

In the *Recollections*, Greeley saw his years of childhood and youth as a blend of both terrible hardship and exciting inspiration. Greeley treated his own past as he had approached the American past in his *American Conflict*, as a time of irrecoverable pleasures and yet lost opportunities. Greeley spoke of the joys of long walks in the wilderness, but he also remembered how that same wilderness had ravaged his mother's health, happiness, and youth. He stressed how his mother suffered in the woods of Western Pennsylvania: "she plunged into the primitive forest too late in life, and never became reconciled to the pioneer's inevitable discomforts. . . . I think the shadow of the great woods oppressed her. I never caught the old smile on her face." While he remembered making charcoal in New England as a tedious task, he also recalled with pleasure watching the green wood burn into charcoal: "To sit or lie in a rude forest—but of boards or logs, . . . and an open, flaring front looking across the fire at the pit, is a pleasant novelty of a wild, quiet evening."[5]

Greeley also traced an ambivalence toward railroads. Remembering how he used to walk from thirty-six to forty-five miles a day, he said that

railroads have nearly killed pedestrianism, and I regret it. Days of steady, solitary, walking I have found most favorable to patient meditation. To study nature profitably, you must be left alone with her,—she does not unveil herself to babbling, shouting crowds. A walk of two or three hundred miles in a calm, clear October, is one of the cheap and wholesome luxuries of life, as free to the poor as the rich.

Yet he also pointed to the miserable travel on boats on the Erie Canal, before railroads were introduced:

And the wretched little tubs that then did duty for steamboats on Lake Erie were scarcely less conducive to the increase and diffusion of human misery. I have suffered in them to the point of mortal endurance. . . . I trust I have due respect for "the good old ways" we often hear of; yet I feel that this earthly life has been practically lengthened and sweetened by the invention and construction of railroads.[6]

Greeley remembered a childhood, which, despite hardships and suffering, nurtured in him those qualities of independence, resilience, curiosity which would be strong resources in adult life. Not the least of important influences was Greeley's Calvinist heritage. Recalling his early years in Londonderry, New Hampshire, Greeley celebrated his Scotch-Irish ancestors who came from Ulster and who had been "rigid Presbyterians" seeking absolute religious freedom "in a land of abundance, an inviting tract of wilderness, known as *Nutfield*," because of the opulence of "chestnut, butternut, and hickory trees." Greeley anticipated modern American historians like Perry Miller in condemning the traditional image of Puritans: "The current notion that the Puritans were a sour, morose, ascetic people—is not justified by my recollection, nor by the tradition handed down through my mother." Greeley also stressed that "there was more humor, more play, more fun, more merriment, in that Puritan community than can be found anywhere in this anxious, plodding age." Greeley recalled a humorous incident when for protection against possible Indian invaders, Puritan ministers carried their guns to "meeting": "Nay, their spiritual teacher and guide for months regularly entered his pulpit musket in hand, and, having cocked it and carefully scrutinized the priming, sat it down in one corner, and devoutly addressed himself to the everlasting God." In a phrase characteristic of his own later life at Chappaqua farm, Greeley spoke of his ancestors' "great tenacity," as they lived a life of "frugal plenty, almost wholly on their own products, spending much of their time in vigorous exercise in the open air."[7]

The impact of the remnants of Calvinism on Greeley came from two cultural traits, his ancestors' life-style and their suspicion about human nature. To Greeley, the community in Londonderry had several ideal features: it was independent, self-sufficient, zestful. Such a model undoubtedly had an influence on Greeley's design for utopian communities in the 1840s. Second, even with his compassion for suffering human beings, Greeley, like Benjamin Franklin, was always aware of human foibles. He liked to contrast his "[morally] diligent, God-fearing" New Hampshire people with the "vices of modern civilization." Indeed, Greeley's moral strictures against divorce, drinking, and smoking drew much from this heritage, and in this sense, he represented later twentieth-century reform movements against similar private "indiscretions."[8]

However, in his chapter, "My Faith," Greeley also showed an early propensity to reject many of the theological tenets of Calvinism. In his chapter on Margaret Fuller, Greeley signaled his admiration for those known as Transcendentalists who had published the *Dial* in 1840, that "small fraternity of scholars and thinkers, who had so far outgrown the recognized standards of orthodox opinion in theology and philosophy." Transcendentalism "indicates an aspiration. . . . Those to whom it was applied had alike transcended the preexisting limitations of decorous and allowable thinking." In his admiration of Ralph Waldo Emerson and in his friendships with Margaret Fuller and Henry David Thoreau, Greeley asserted his empathy with their pattern of rebellion, an empathy derived from his own religious reflections. For Greeley was a basically optimistic and humanitarian thinker. He trusted that "all suffering is disciplinary and transitional, and shall ultimately result in universal holiness and consequent happiness."[9]

Said Greeley in Emersonian fashion, "In the light of this faith, the dark problem of Evil is irrational, and virtually solved." Declaring himself an Universalist, Greeley perceived the limitations of his faith: "I am not wise enough, even in my own conceit, to assume to say where and when the deliverance of our race from evil and suffering shall be consummated." Greeley drew from Alfred Tennyson's *In*

Memoriam to illustrate his faith in an eventual deliverance, yet his rendering was notably selective, for while he accurately quoted, "I can but trust that good shall fall / At last,—far off—at last to all, / And every Winter change to Spring," he neglected to insert Tennyson's last, cryptic stanza, "So runs my dream, but what am I / An infant crying in the night, / An infant crying for the light, / And with no language but a cry."[10]

Despite admiration for his past, Greeley also recalled the ugliness of his father's poverty, which caused the family to move several times in search of prosperity. Greeley stated that he had as a youth made the "acquaintance of genuine poverty—not beggary nor dependence, but the manly American sort."[11] After Greeley left the family to become an apprentice printer, his father had sought sustenance in the wilderness. But the memory of his mother's struggle decimated any romantic notions Greeley might have entertained about a pioneer's life.

Disliking the rather crude implements and methods used on his farm, Greeley felt caught. He learned the value of agricultural education, what he would always call "scientific farming" and what other farmers would derisively designate as "book" farming. Concerning farming in Westhaven, Vermont, Greeley said, "I never saw a book that treated of Agriculture and the natural sciences. . . . I think I never saw even one copy of a periodical devoted mainly to farming. . . . I know I had the stuff in me for an efficient and successful farmer, but such training as I received at home would never have brought it out."[12]

At this point, Greeley introduced a central theme in his personal philosophy, the necessity of intellectual freedom. To him, the physical movement westward meant nothing if it did not represent a sense of spiritual release. Men and women left farming in droves not just because of a lack of economic opportunity, but because of cultural stagnation:

Our farmers' sons escape from their father's calling whenever they can, because it is made a mindless, monotonous drudgery, instead of an ennobling liberalizing, intellectual pursuit. . . . In the farmer's calling, . . . there was neither scope for expanding facilities, incitement to constant growth in knowledge, nor a spur to generous ambition. To preserve existence was its ordinary impulse, to get rich, its exceptional and most exalted aim. So I turned from it in dissatisfaction, if not in disgust, and sought a different sphere and vocation.[13]

Indeed, according to the *Recollections,* Greeley developed an intellectual curiosity early in life. Despite his erratic formal schooling, he devoured whatever books came his way and showed a brilliance for spelling and reading before the age of eight. Parton inteviewed a man who had driven the Greeley family to their new home in Westhaven, Vermont: "The teamster remembers well the intelligent, white-headed boy who was so pressing with his questions, as they rode along over the snow, and who soon exhausted the man's knowledge of the geography of the region in which he had lived all his days."[14] Greeley reminisced how a group of neighbors in New Hampshire had been so impressed with his scholarship that they were willing to fund his education at Phillips Exeter Academy, an offer which, Greeley noted in a somewhat self-serving statement, his parents wisely rejected.

III *Journalism*

When Greeley, at the age of fifteen, left his family to begin his apprenticeship in East Poultney, he was introduced to two influences which would broaden his cultural awareness, the art of writing and the development of a newspaper. In the *Recollections,* Greeley stated that as a printer for the *Northern Spectator,* he had learned the value of concision in writing. Working from city newspapers, he learned to improve "not only in the selection, but in the condensation, of news . . . and afterward as a printer of sundry experimental journals in the city, so that I began my distinctive, avowed editorial career in The New-Yorker with a considerable experience as a writer of articles and paragraphs."[15]

In East Poultney, Greeley began to discover the role for which he would become famous: a dispenser of information, with judicious commentary, to people in all callings. The role of a great newspaper, Greeley acknowledged, was to keep citizens informed so that democracy could function. Said Greeley,

We need to know, not only what is done, but what is purposed and said, by those who sway the destinies of states and realms; and, to this end, the prompt perusal of the manifests of monarchs, presidents, ministers, legislators, . . . is indispensable. No man is ever totally informed . . . who does not regularly "keep the run" of events and opinions, through the daily perusal of at least *one* good journal, and the ready cavil that "no one can read" all that a great modern journal contains only proves the ignorance or thoughtlessness of the caviller.

While admitting that no one person could possibly cover the contents of an entire newspaper, Greeley advocated selective, creative reading: "The idea is rather to embody in a single sheet the information daily required by all those who aim to keep posted on every important occurrence, so that the lawyer, . . . merchant, . . . banker, . . . farmworker, . . . economist, . . . author, . . . politician . . . may find here whatever he needs to see, and be spared the trouble of looking elsewhere."[16] In another famous tract, *A Dissertation in the Canon and Feudal Law*, John Adams had cited the necessity of a free press to keep check on the passions and proclivitives of rulers. Said Adams,

Liberty cannot be preserved without a general knowledge among the people, who have a right . . . to that most dreaded and envied kind of knowledge—I mean, of the characters and conduct of their rulers . . . none of the means of information are more sacred or have been cherished with more tenderness and care by the settlers of America than the press.

For Greeley, the move to East Poultney established his commitment to journalism, and when he sought a more permanent position in the news business, he recorded how he left the town, first for a short stay in Erie, Pennsylvania, where he worked for the *Erie Gazette,* and then for the move to New York City in 1831, where he gained limited employment for the *Evening Post.* As with so many American country boys and girls in the nineteenth and early twentieth centuries, Greeley found the city a place of opportunity and intellectual stimulation. Through his political and business associations in New York, he would edit his first newspapers and establish the *New York Tribune.* As Greeley said, despite his "rustic manner and address . . . the world was all before me."[17]

IV Poverty

But if New York opened Greeley's life to new dimensions of experience, it also represented, particularly with the Depression of 1837, a recurrence of the poverty of his early youth, albeit in an urban setting. As Greeley said after the *Tribune* was first issued, he was now on a more secure financial basis and was released at last from stringent circumstances; the "transition from my four preceding years of incessant pecuniary anxiety if not absolute embarrassment, was like escaping from the dungeon and the rack to freedom and sympathy." Greeley's own experience with poverty further awakened his commitment to the dispossessed, a commitment evident in some editorials issued in the 1830s and 1840s in which he argued for his own variety of socialism, unlike European manifestations. As he said in *Hints Toward Reforms*, Greeley understood that freedom in America meant little without freedom from want. The first half of the *Recollections* was filled with Dickensian images of human beings caught in an endless cycle of poverty. As Greeley compassionately stated, "Mechanics and laborers of every moderate ability, and even widows with small children, hie hither, in reckless defiance of the fact that myriads have done so before them,—at least nineteenth-twentieths of them only to plunge thereby into deeper, more squalid, hopeless misery than they had previously known."[18]

Greeley's vision anticipated those of Henry George and Upton Sinclair:

Want is a hard master anywhere, but nowhere else are the sufferings, the woes, the desperation, of utter need so trying as in a great city; and they are preeminently so in *this* city, because the multiplicity of the destitute benumbs the heart of charity and precludes attention to any one's wants, while each is absorbed in his own cares and efforts to such extent that he knows nothing of the neighbors who may be starving to death, with barely a brick wall between him and them.

In the winter of 1837–1838, Greeley saw

destitution more closely than I had even before observed it, and was enabled to scan its repulsive features intelligently. I saw two families, including six or eight children, burrowing in one cellar under a stable,—a prey to famine on one hand, and to vermin and cutaneous maladies on the other, with sickness adding its horrors to those of a polluted atmosphere and a wintry temperature. . . . I saw three widows, with as many children, living in an attic on the profits of an apple-stand which yielded less than $3 per week.

Mentioning his friendship with the Utopian Socialist, Albert Brisbane, Greeley underlined his faith that progress could alleviate poverty rather than create it:

We may so provide that labor, now repulsive, shall be attractive; while its efficiency in production shall be increased by the improvement of machinery and the extended use of natural forces, so as to secure abundance, education, and elegant luxury, to all. What is needed is to provide all with houses, employment, instruction, good living, the most effective implements, machinery . . . , serving to each the faith and full recompense of his achievement.

To Greeley, this could be fulfilled through the development of what he termed "association," through "four to five hundred families in a common household, and in the ownership and cultivation of a common domain, say of 2,000 acres, or about one acre to each person living thereon."[19]

Greeley's "New Deal" socialism contained eight tenets: civilization paid a higher price for unemployment than would the cost of its eradication; there was no excuse for national unemployment, as what was lacking was not capital, but imagination to devise useful work; inefficiency in industrial management was a cause of unemployment; inefficiency in production was equaled by "waste in consumption"; children needed an education in industrial skills as much as in letters and sciences; isolation for an individual or community, separating them from the national stimulus, benefited no one; the poor remained poor precisely because they were poor; a communitarian association would overcome economic isolation and release men and women to a more rewarding use of leisure time in the arts.[20]

As in *Hints Toward Reforms*, Greeley's writing was strongest in his discussions of poverty. Many of his ideas had a modernist tone, suggesting how much the nineteenth-century reform movement of the 1840s, in its milder forms, still instructed and engaged the liberalism of twentieth-century America. Greeley's concern with efficiency, unemployment, spiritual isolation, and vocational education does not seem much different from similar concerns in the 1980s.

V   *Margaret Fuller and Henry Clay*

In the first half of the *Recollections*, Greeley paused to pay tribute to two persons who made a deep impact on his maturing life, Henry Clay and Margaret Fuller. A man's choice of heroes is revealing, and in a sense, Clay remained a model for Greeley's public aspirations while Fuller represented an ideal for his private, spiritual search. Of course, Greeley fully endorsed Clay's nationalism, his American system, his gradual approach to emancipation, his support of the high tariff. He worked hard for Clay's election in 1844, and was deeply disappointed at Clay's failure once again to gain the coveted prize. While he did not personally know Clay well, he was impressed with his forensic skill, his ability to unite the Whig party, his commitment to the nation. In Clay, as did Lincoln, Greeley saw something of himself. He noted how Clay was the classic example of an American success story. Clay, "born in poverty and obscurity," had largely self-educated himself for his illustrious career. Greeley stressed how

Clay's "fervid patriotism and thrilling eloquence combined with decided natural abilities and a wide and varied experience to render him
the American more fitted to win and enjoy popularity than any other
who has lived."[21] In a sense, Greeley anticipated his own hopes for
his presidential effort four years later. Like Clay, Greeley would
preach national unity and attempt to draw upon the good will of the
American people for his campaign. And like Clay, he would fail.

But if Clay emerged as Greeley's model for the person of political
power, Margaret Fuller became an inspiration for another kind of
power, intellectual power, the ability to shape men's and women's
minds. Greeley stated that when Fuller lived with his family in New
York City in the 1840s, she would converse brilliantly with groups of
women who visited her: "her magnetic sway over these was marvell-
ous, inaccountable." She undoubtedly had a deep impact on his own
ideas of the women's place in American society. He termed her work,
Woman in the Nineteenth Century, the "clearest . . . most logical . . .
loftiest and most commanding assertion . . . made of the right of
Woman to be regarded and treated as an independent, intelligent,
rational being, entitled to an equal voice in framing and modifying the
laws she is required to obey, and in controlling and disposing of the
property she has inherited or aided to acquire." In his introduction to
this book, published six years after her death, Greeley, taking the
voice of woman, asked rhetorically, "In short, why am I not regarded
by the law as a *soul*, responsible for my acts to God and humanity and
not as a mere lady, devoted to the unreasoning service of my husband?" He stressed Fuller's commitment to the emancipation of all
women, rich and poor, and declared that with her untimely death in a
shipwreck off Long Island, "So passed away the loftiest, bravest soul
that has yet irradicated the form of an American woman."[22]

In a sense, Greeley wanted Fuller's kind of power. He wished to be
educator as well as manipulator, a stimulus to the way people think as
well as how they act. When, in his great editorials, Greeley was able
to render the force of his best ideas as justification for certain actions,
he was often highly persuasive. But too frequently, his quests for
political power denied his best, transcendent self. In a revealing
moment in the *Recollections*, Greeley hinted at this limitation when
he recognized that his role as editor of the *Tribune*, where he could
enrich his editorials with his own distinctive commentary, was his
most significant contribution to public life. As an editor, he could be,
like his good friend Margaret Fuller, magnetic, convincing his un-
seen audience of millions just as she was so persuasive in her private
conversations in Greeley's home. Said Greeley, fame

is a vapor, popularity an accident, riches takes wings, the only certainty is oblivion, no man can foresee what a day may bring forth, . . . And yet I cherish the hope that the journal I projected and established will live and flourish long after I shall have mouldered into forgotten dust, being guided by a larger wisdom, a more unerring sagacity to discern the right, though not by a more unfaltering readiness to embrace and defend it at whatever personal cost, and that the stone which covers my ashes may bear to future eyes the still intelligible inscription, "Founder of the New York Tribune."[23]

Much of the second half of Greeley's *Recollections* covered his public career as an editor, congressman, politician, Republican, tourist, presidential candidate—material reported in other writings. He spoke of his opposition to the Mexican War and Kansas-Nebraska Act, first made explicit in his editorials and later in *The American Conflict*. He spoke of his support of the Union and yet of peace initiatives in the Civil War and of his mixed views of Abraham Lincoln. He covered his trips to Europe in 1851 and 1855 and his own venture into the Far West, journeys fully reported in *Glances at Europe* and *Overland Journey*.

But in this portion of the *Recollections* as well as the early part, Greeley's commitment was clear: emancipation from all varieties of bondage. His self-portrait remained a memorable creation of a questing American mind which reached beyond the normal limits of nineteenth-century experience and yet retained the faith of that era. As Greeley stated, "The true Eden lies before, not behind us."[24] That the dream had not died was indicated by Thomas Wolfe's similar prophecy so many years later in *You Can't Go Home Again*, "The true discovery of America lies before us."

CHAPTER 8

Final Reflections

I Political Economy

IN HIS later years, which marked an energetic outpouring of books, Greeley defined his economic thinking more clearly. In 1869, he published his *Essays Designed to Elucidate the Science of Political Economy,* which became the credo of his economic thought. Greeley's study illustrated economic principles which he had espoused all his life, a benevolent capitalism, the protective tariff, and the policy of cooperation between workers and owners of capital. The subtitle underlined these commitments: "While Serving to Explain and Defend the Policy of Protection to Home Industry, as a System of National Cooperation for the Elevation of Labor." Greeley appropriately dedicated his polemic to the memory of the founder of the American system, Henry Clay, and Greeley said he "aimed in his writing to be lucid and simple."[1]

Greeley's book, influenced by the thought of Henry Carey, was a good text for an understanding of nineteenth-century economics, but it served mainly as a restatement of the ideals of an updated version of the American system. Greeley was devoted to developing as strong a self-sufficient national economic system as possible; rather than viewing the protective tariff as "narrow-minded" and disruptive of international harmony, Greeley felt that the United States could best benefit countries less physically endowed by first concentrating on strengthening national wealth and then sharing that treasure with developing nations: as he said, the "true, beneficent relation of the more advanced . . . to the less developed . . . industries of diverse nations seems to be one of friendly encouragement, not depressing, destructive competition."[2] However, with the support of the tariff, Greeley seemed to sponsor competition first and cooperation thereafter. Yet Greeley thought the tariff would aid all economic classes, including farmers and laborers, by guaranteeing both satisfactory prices and sufficient wages. Also, the consumer would not suffer because protection increased the number of domestic competitors who would reduce prices on a given product. Furthermore, Greeley gave a place for labor unions, which, he asserted, deserved a status equal to any other industrial agency. In this fashion, Greeley, while often lauding capitalistic enterprise, was not committed solely to industrial management. In a period when national officials are calling for national independence in energy, Greeley's advice is modern.

Just as in the 1830s and 1840s, albeit less utopian, Greeley remained committed to a version of economic democracy in which all participants, the producers or laborers and the managers, could share in ownership and decision making. As in *Hints Toward Reform,* he defined this economic democracy as cooperation, "the organization of workmen into bodies capable of selling their own labor or its product by wholesale, and fairly dividing or allotting its proceeds, or of consumers to purchase in gross whatever they may require, and divide or apportion it at the least possible cost." This appeared to Greeley to be "the step next ahead in the industrial and social progress of the civilized world."[3]

Despite the congenial nature of Greeley's economic vision, it possessed illusory conceptions. He could not explain away the reality that the high tariff virtually guaranteed a competitive international structure, one which could lead to political instability and conflict. Also, his stance on cooperation overlooked a fact which he knew and even relished in daily life: that economic interest groups were bound to clash even in a highly moral capitalistic nation.

While rejoicing in the "industrial achievement" of the nation, Greeley stated that the "rights of those who create Intellectual Property are less clearly defined."[4] Here he introduced a moving appeal for international copyright, which would protect authors and reward them for their special labors.

II *Agriculture*

As Glyndon Van Deusen has shown, Horace Greeley's advice about agriculture in his editorials and other writings was often wise. While in his *Recollections* Greeley had shown no regrets about abandoning farming as an occupation, he remained interested in it as an avocation. Greeley's purchase of his farm in Chappaqua, New York, represented more than an opportunity to pursue one of his favorite hobbies; it was a return to the resources of his own heritage, a return to a relationship with the land which had initially shaped his youth. He devoted two chapters of his *Recollections* to his activities in farming. As Greeley confessed,

I should have been a farmer. . . . Its quiet, its segregation from strife, and brawls, and heated rivalries attract and delight me. I hate to earn my bread in any calling which complicates my prosperity in some sort with others' adversity—my success with others' defeat . . . were I to begin my life anew, I would choose to earn my bread by cultivating the soil. Blessed is he whose day's exertion ends with the evening twilight, and who can sleep unbrokenly and without anxiety till the dawn awakes him, with energies renewed and senses brightened, to fresh activity and that fullness of health and vigor which one vouchsafed to those only who spend most of their waking hours in the free, pure air and renovating sunshine of the open country.[5]

Greeley's experiments with various agricultural techniques and his eagerness to show others the results of his efforts indicated his conviction that his farm could be an educational laboratory for others. Always an advocate of agricultural education and scientific farming, Greeley certainly was an agricultural pioneer in an era which witnessed the founding of the first land-grant college at what is now Michigan State University in 1855 and the passage of the Morrill Act in 1862, inaugurating a national plan for land-grant colleges.

The summation of his ideas on agriculture appeared in the last of his full-length books, *What I Know of Farming,* which was published in 1871. This work remained one of the clearest, most precise books he ever penned, partially because he wrote it, as he said in the conclusion, in a systematic manner, unlike the more hurried works of earlier days. He devised one chapter every week in the year of 1870, despite illness and demanding editorial and political responsibilities. Because Greeley wrote so well in shorter forms, each of the fifty-two chapters had a crispness lacking in other books, and yet each was sufficiently interwoven with the total work so as to present a sustained narrative. While the book was filled with solid practical advice, much of it still current, on such problems as pollution, irrigation, pasturing, use of fertilizers, the growth of orchards, the importance of trees, it also contained fine examples of Greeley's philosophy from the perspective of sixty years of life. The sense of a self-commemorative was reinforced by the fact that he wrote his introduction on February 3, 1871, his sixtieth birthday.

While Greeley declared in the *Recollections* that he never had an aversion to the ax, and while at times he appeared to be just one more representative of the nineteenth-century attitude of exploiting the land for human purposes, Greeley's conception proved to be more complex. He was susceptible to the beauty of his natural environment and was an early advocate of the conservation movement. For instance, in *What I Know of Farming*, Greeley said he was not sentimental about the destruction of trees; he viewed them as instruments of utility, not mere ornaments. Yet, he stated, "I am not insensitive to the beauty and grace lent by woods and groves, and clumps or rows of trees, the landscape they diversify. I feel the force of Emerson's comment that 'Beauty is an excuse for Being.' "[6]

Furthermore, Greeley argued that cultivation must be a learned, selective procedure. Again he returned to a sense of balance. In discussing forestry in the *Recollections*, he argued that any "fairly grown forest can always spare trees, and be benefited by their removal." But he "protested" against the practice of "cutting off and burning over our forests," an example of "reckless waste": "In regions which are all woods, ground must of course be cleared for cultivation, but many a founder goes on slashing and burning long after he should halt and begin . . . saving his timber." Greeley gave advice not much different from that used today in restoring arid land. He said that with

one fourth of your land in wood, judiciously covering the rest of your ridges, the sides of your ravines, your farms will grow more grass than if wholly denuded and laid bare to the scorching sun. Protracted, desolating drouths, bleak, scathing winds, and the failure of delicate fruits like peach and finer pears, are part of the penalty we pay for depriving our fields and gardens of the genial, hospitable protection of forests.

In an earlier part of the *Recollections*, Greeley anticipated the national and state parks movement by advocating that portions of the Catskills Mountains in New York and the Poconos in Pennsylvania be

converted into spacious deer-parks . . . [and] planted with the best timber, and held by large companies of shareholders for sporting, under proper regulation. A century hence, those bleak mountains . . . would be covered, as of old, with a magnificent forest, containing more serviceable pine than is now standing in all our states east of the Potomac and Lake Erie.[7]

But if Greeley were farseeing in his commitment to conservation, he was also bound by a narrow focus in terms of the livelihood of farming. In some ways, he overlooked the poverty of his rural youth and insisted that farming, with proper conservationist techniques, could "pay." He asserted the New England bias that a farmer could obtain "a position of independence, comfort, and comparative leisure." Yet, in a realistic sense, Greeley recognized farming as a "business in which success is nearly certain as in this,"[8] while he valued "association" in farming as well as in labor because he felt that individuals could become self-dependent. He evoked a contradiction which, as Richard Hofstadter has demonstrated, characterized some Populist rhetoric later: that the call for the agrarian ideal distorted the reality that farming was deeply dependent on the forces of the international economy over which producers had often little control. With their programs for more direct government intervention in the agricultural process, Populists, despite their rhetoric, understood new realities of dependency which Greeley clearly could not have anticipated.

III   The West and Blacks

But this was not to say that Greeley was fundamentally simplistic in defining his ideal of the farming experience. In his advice about where to farm, Greeley again showed the complexity of his approach to the West belied by the slogan "Go West, young man." Like Crèvecoeur, Greeley displayed a distaste for the wilderness; he criticized the "class of drinking, hunting, fishing, rarely working" men who lived on the frontier. The East still had abundant fertile land. Yet with a Turneresque vision, Greeley remained committed to frontier development, not only in the West but in the South as well:

And yet I believe in migration—believe that there are thousands in the Eastern and Middle Western States who would improve their circumstances and prospects by migrating to the cheaper lands and broader opportunities of the West and South. For, in the first place, most men are by migration rendered more energetic and aspiring; thrown among strangers, they feel the necessity of exertion as they never felt it before. Needing almost everything and obliged to rely wholly on themselves, they work in their new homes as they never did in their old, and the consequences are soon visible all around them.[9]

Greeley particularly encouraged American blacks now "subsisting by servile labor in cities, to strike out boldly for homes of their own." For Greeley, if, as he said in the preface, the great achievement of his age was aiding "The banishment of human chattelhood from our soil," this did not mean that blacks need be emancipated from the soil.[10]

For Greeley had deep compassion for blacks who had to struggle for survival in the cities. Even whites had trouble. Greeley punctured the myth that the city always represented new opportunities. Perhaps young men should remain on the farms. Greeley spoke of the "great difficulties encountered by every poor young man in securing a good start in life." He recalled how he had arrived in New York City with good health, a solid elementary education, a good trade. Still, he needed ten years to overcome "adverse" circumstances, even after he had followed all of the prescriptions of the Protestant ethic: hard work and avoiding drinking, smoking, extravagant "entertainments."[11]

Despite his emphasis on the individualism of the farmer, Greeley did not abandon earlier commitments to voluntary commutarianism. In a Populist refrain, he advised cooperation, a sharing of technological instruments, labor resources, knowledge, and land. He differentiated his kind of rural socialism from Marxist communism by insisting that each person should receive "what he had earned" rather than a guaranteed allotment dependent on the size of his family.[12]

By advising young men to become pioneer farmers, Greeley returned to his own conception of the necessity of economic freedom. In the city, Greeley had witnessed too many incidents of the miseries of suppressed labor. His solution, the "escape valves" of the West and the South, was at once too utopian, unrealistic, ill advised. Yet Greeley ultimately was concerned with the psychological well-being of his fellows. Here he was accurate. Away from the competitive struggle of the city, men and women could achieve self-respect and purpose again. The pioneer "would grow year by year into a . . . firmer conviction that short-sighted selfishness is the germ of half the evils that afflict the human race. and that the true and sure way to a bounteous satisfaction of the wants of each is a generous and thoughtful consideration for the needs of all."[13]

That kind of talk illustrated the basis for Greeley's appeal for so many years. After all, Greeley's America was still largely rural, and he possessed the capacity to transgress the limits between city and country in a persuasive way for his audience. They could sense that the ideals of the boy who "made good in the city" had not succumbed to urban corruption; he could still speak for them.

CHAPTER 9

The Campaigner

I *Power and Principle*

IN 1872, Horace Greeley returned to his passion for power and began his last quest for an official capacity worthy of his national reputation. He was nominated for the presidency both by the Liberal Republican movement and the Democratic party. While Greeley had sometimes disparaged the idea of running for president in the past, he now eagerly welcomed the challenge. There was no question that he coveted the glory of the office, but, to his credit, he also deeply believed that he could help unite and heal a nation still recovering from the ravages of an immense civil war, whose history he had recounted in *The American Conflict.* He did not succumb to the ecstacy of power, but instead, as indicated in all his writing, he hoped to use power to elevate the nation to the high plane of his own principles.

With brilliant insight, historian John R. Commons has argued that Greeley was committed to a "higher idealism" rather than a "lower idealism." Said Commons, the "lower [idealism] was class-conscious, aggressive, coercive," while to Greeley the "higher idealism was humanitarian, harmonizing, persuasive. . . . The higher was a plea for justice: the lower a demand for rights." Said Commons, what Greeley offered "was a socialism of class harmony, not one of class struggle."[1]

As his postwar book publications suggested, Greeley also had entered a more reflective period of his life, and while he had supported Ulysses Grant for president in 1868, he agreed with many of his Liberal Republican associates that Grant's administration had failed to unite the nation and to achieve the necessary restoration requested in Lincoln's second inaugural address. Because of his demonstrated commitments to various regions of the nation, Greeley thought he was the one person who could appeal to the full country. In this, of course, he was mistaken.

To buttress his concerns, Greeley made a significant contribution to campaign literature when he went on tour in September. While the relevance of such rhetoric has often been doubted, Greeley's speeches underlined once again the significance of the public debate over the vital issues of that contest. A fuller exploration of the public considerations is needed to comprehend Greeley's special oratory.

II *National Unity*

The concern over national unity in the 1980s prompts a reexamination of the impact the American Civil War had on postbellum attempts to redefine the nation. Greeley knew Americans emerged from that conflict bewildered and confused. Each of the campaigns from 1860 to 1876 highlighted an internal crisis of spirit, from secession to war to reunion. And each crisis accented a debate over the meaning of the nation. And no one better contributed to this debate than Greeley.

Prior to the Civil War, Americans did not link nationalism exclusively with political power. Like Greeley, they emphasized their sense of an open democratic community. By the 1870s the strain of war and reconstruction had shattered the common national commitments displayed in 1860. Not only was national sentiment considerably weakened; it now was split between two different views of the nation, the nation as community and as nation-state. As a presidential candidate, Greeley attempted to reconcile these perspectives.

The image of unity and power which America displayed to the world in 1872 was impressive, but in the continued bitterness of Reconstruction, Americans were still struggling to recapture that sense of antebellum unity. With a growing civilian bureaucracy and military establishment, a new industrialism, and new developments in transportation and communications, Americans had created the machinery for a strong nation, but the necessary devotion was missing. In the latter half of the 1860s the newly completed transcontinental railroad symbolized the new economic integration and industrial power. Secretary of State William H. Seward's vindication of the Monroe Doctrine in Mexico and his acquisition of Alaska signaled a new international power. A Republican wartime governor of Illinois, Richard Yates, boasted that "we are scarcely known in foreign countries as states but as a great nation." A Republican congressman from Massachusetts, George F. Hoar, exalted the nation's potential empire.[2] But this confidence was a mask which concealed national disorientation.

In many ways, Greeley, with his support of industrialism and a national railroad, had sponsored the new America. But, like others, he worried about the nation's spirit and whether, in a new age, America could preserve the best values of its democratic heritage.

For by 1872, Americans had had seven years to reflect on the war's meaning, and many orators, regardless of political persuasion, still emphasized the waste, death, and destruction. Many saw the war leading directly to the demoralization and scandals of the Ulysses Grant administration. Hence a major theme of some political rhetoric was the Civil War as a failure, which had destroyed the American people's primary commitment to the nation. In 1860, many Americans had felt deep impulses of national sentiment and lacked the technological means to forge a mighty nation; now they possessed the means but had lost the impetus. Because the war had ended slavery, Greeley, unlike others, never felt the war had failed in its greatest purpose; but he showed his deep concern over the unhappy results of Reconstruction.

Orators of all parties agreed about the disruption of the war. Some of the Republican idealism of the 1860s had lost its force, especially after their Reconstruction program had apparently failed. The Liberal Republicans, who joined the Democrats during the campaign, employed the theme of civil war more for the purpose of reunion than for political victory. Greeley expressed the desire to "clasp hands across the bloody chasm" opened up by the Civil War, and during his campaign travels he spoke of its awesome trials and bloody destruction.[3]

The question of rekindling national sentiment after the calamity became the main debate of the 1872 presidential campaign, where arguments went beyond personalities and issues to a discussion of America's future. Divergent views of the nation tended to polarize around opposing political parties. Americans had not only a choice between parties and issues, but between concepts of the nation's mission as well. The two definitions of nationality which had first appeared during the Civil War continued to dominate the rhetoric. One view, supported mainly by old Northern and Midwestern Grant Republicans, was revolutionary: as in 1864 and 1868, it demanded a militant nationalism created not by individual will but by centralized geographic, political, and economic institutions. Republicans believed that technical contrivances would ensure future national power. And President Grant stressed this message in his 1873 inaugural address.[4] Republicans emphasized centralism as a means to integrate forcefully a large country like the United States. This was something new for Americans, but Republicans hoped that a clever elite of centralist leaders could realize national commitments. They offered the American people a new nationalism, the wave of a not too distant future, and they hoped to join it to a reawakened national consciousness.

The opposite conception of nationality, sponsored by both Democrats and Liberal Republicans, would restore antebellum Democratic nationalism. Nationalism was a voluntary, popular emotion impervious to central institutions or powerful, governing cliques. According to the Liberal platform, "local self-government . . . will guard the rights of all citizens more securely than any centralized power." The nation must "return to the methods of peace and the constitutional limitations of power." Democrats and Liberals regarded nationalism as a powerful moral force, which brought goodness and freedom in its westward spread. National impulses must spring from the hearts of the people. To achieve unity, most people must feel these impulses simultaneously. The government had inadvertently controlled or channeled these impulses by force, which only served to inhibit or destroy unity. Nationalism had to be achieved by the common consent of willing subjects. These orators sought to obliterate the Civil War from memory and revive the traditional nationalism crushed by the war.

Greeley's own attitude toward federal governmental power had always been ambivalent. As an exponent of Clay's American system, he differed from his fellow Liberal and Democratic campaigners in that he advocated centrist power to help the disadvantaged and economic development. This was why he had supported a vigorous governmental prosecution of the Civil War from 1861 to 1865 and why he had introduced a homestead bill as a congressman. But he had always been suspicious about the potential abuse of individual rights; he believed in dissent; he saw the virtue of decentralization in some cases; and these concerns surfaced during the campaign.

III *Liberal Republicans*

The debate on the national mission was largely molded in 1872 by the dissenting Liberal Republicans. The Liberal Republican movement gave the campaign its peculiar distinction and helped embellish the earlier arguments of 1864 and 1868 with more precision. The movement began in Missouri in 1870 under the leadership of two leading Republicans, Senator Carl Schurz and Governor B. Gratz Brown, in reaction to regular Republican policies. Calling for a "New Departure," the dissidents achieved national recognition as an anti-Grant movement, gaining the eventual support of such outstanding leaders as Lyman Trumbull, George Julian, and Charles Sumner. Liberal Republicans were dissatisfied with Grant's high tariff policy, his vindictive Southern policy, his corrupt misuse of federal patronage, and his imperialistic foreign policy. In some cases there were also personal antagonisms. Grant embittered Charles Sumner, for instance, forcing him out of the chairmanship of the Senate Committee on Foreign Relations because of his opposition to the annexation of Santo Domingo. Grant's apparent abandonment of peace and reform also upset Schurz, Trumbull, and Julian. Henry Adams's caustic description of Grant as a man lacking ideas or moral force aptly stated the Liberals' attitude.

For stretches of time, his mind seemed torpid. . . . He should have been extinct for ages. That . . . a man like Grant should be called . . . the highest product of the most advanced evolution, made evolution ludicrous. One must be as commonplace as Grant's own commonplaces to maintain such an absurdity.[5]

As for Reconstruction failures, Liberals stressed the theme of reconciliation through William M. Stewart's original 1866 plan of universal suffrage and universal amnesty.[6] The Fifteenth Amendment, supporting the impartial suffrage, was a step toward the former in 1870, and Liberals sought congressional legislation that would guarantee the latter. To them, Grant's Amnesty Act of May 22, 1872, was inadequate because it was a political measure aimed at undercutting the Liberal program. It was also incomplete, omitting 500 ex-Confederates. In addition, Liberals called for civil service reform and free trade as means of resuming the progress of the antebellum period. The Liberals' platform advocated acceptance of the Thirteenth, Fourteenth, and Fifteenth Amendments as accomplished facts.

The Liberal Republicans' convention met at Cincinnati on May 1 and named as its president Carl Schurz, who delivered the keynote address, "The Aims of the Liberal Republicans." Schurz characterized the movement as a peaceful revolution of the people, whose aroused national conscience had reacted against a corrupt Grant era which threatened the national strength. After approving a platform consistent with Schurz's opening charge, the convention shocked the nation with its selection of Greeley over such favorites as Ambassador Charles Francis Adams, Judge David Davis, Senator Lyman Trumbull, and former Pennsylvania Governor Andrew Curtin. Behind the upset lay a pro-Greeley speech by one of the prominent candidates, Benjamin Gratz Brown, help from a powerful Midwestern newspaper clique led by Murat Halstead of Cincinnati, and Greeley's national reputation. The choice of Brown as the second half of the ticket increased suspicions of a bargain in the party of pristine purity. Schurz personally favored Adams and feared he had lost control of the movement. Greeley's vacillating past record as a Republican was distasteful to Schurz, and he let Greeley know it. Yet in his opening address, Schurz emphasized the nationalism of Liberal Republicans by noting that the "patriotic citizen rises above the partisan" in joining the movement and that the "summons is resounding North and South and East and West. The conscience of the people, which seemed dead, had arisen." Greeley's brilliant conduct as a campaigner would show that no one could have been a better champion of Schurz's ideas. The Democrats, including the South, met in Baltimore on July 9 and by prearrangement endorsed the Liberal platform and candidates.[7]

Greeley was a peculiar candidate for the Liberal Republican and Democratic parties. At first a supporter of Grant, he had not broken from him until 1871. Furthermore, his consistent support of a high tariff made his candidacy an embarrassment to a movement which supported free trade, and his endorsement of a constitutional amendment for a single term presidency suggested he was running against the office. The manner of his nomination carried overtones of a political deal. Greeley's past, especially his erratic course during the Civil War, was a liability.

Greeley's personal appearance also made him an easy subject for ridicule. Thomas Nast's savage cartoons in *Harper's Weekly* depicted a short, plumpish man wearing a white coat, steel spectacles, and a white hat barely concealing a crop of frazzled white hair. Greeley looked like an effeminate, wild-eyed fanatic. Nast's portrait, caricature though it was, must have impressed many voters, for, indeed, Greeley in real life did lack the dignified appearance of a president. Greeley's supporters attempted to transform his oddities of appearance into affectionate emblems. They called him "Old White Hat," "Old Honesty," "Old White Coat," and "Farmer of Chappaqua."

Edward A. Pollard presented a sympathetic treatment, comparing
Greeley to Polonius of William Shakespeare's *Hamlet:*

And by the way, is there not a striking likeness of character between the "sage
of Chappaqua" and this wise old Polonius, who, with all that is laughable
about him and the simplicity of character that the prince twits, has yet such
sage and genial philosophy in his sleeve, and despite all his eccentricities is
yet by far the kindest-hearted and the wisest-minded man in the Court of
Denmark.[8]

IV *Republicans*

The Republicans met on June 5 and renominated Grant with a new
vice-presidential candidate, Henry Wilson of Massachusetts, an
abolitionist who could appeal to Liberal Republicans. The platform
celebrated past Republican triumphs and praised the president.[9]
Grant's record as a diplomat, as a champion of blacks, and as an
advocate of civil service, seemed stronger than it would a year later.
In a way, Grant Republicans were more realistic in their assessment
of nationalism than their opponents. They agreed that the Civil War
had destroyed the old nationalism, but they regarded that destruction as irreversible and proposed to create something new out of the
powerful ensuing centralization. Their theme was innovation. Democrats hoped to loosen institutional restraints created by the Civil
War and return to the old nationalism. In the end, as in 1864 and 1868,
these Republican-Democrat disagreements proved more important
than any consensus. The fusion of so many Northern Liberal Republicans with Northern and Southern Democrats illustrated deep
cleavages across the nation. An examination of the political rhetoric of
each side reveals that these divisions were not exclusively a function
of regional allegiances.

Republican rhetoric celebrated a forceful, militant nationalism
represented by the emergent nation-state. Some of the idealistic zeal
had been lost during the Grant years, thanks to political maneuvering
in the party between the party stalwarts and the half-breeds. Stalwarts supported the spoils system and Grantism. Half-breeds
favored some mild reforms. Both groups wished to control the
party, indicating more concern with partisan power than with the
national welfare. But both groups remained loyal to the president and
the regular organization. Although their enthusiasm had waned, both
embraced a similar idea of nationalism.

Their common nationalist doctrine stressed government paternalism, and government as a protective force for blacks, especially in the South. As in previous campaigns, Republicans belittled the concept of state sovereignty. Nationalism and states' rights, which the platform had fused in 1860, were no longer compatible.

Grant Republicans emphasized the beneficence of their new nationalism. Despite their paternalism, Republicans outlined a humanitarian concept of the nation-state sufficiently broad enough to comprise a conglomerate of peoples from diverse ethnic and racial backgrounds. Early conceptions of nationalism had lacked the discipline of order. Eager to avoid new fissures in American society, Republicans sponsored a form of nationalism in which control and freedom would coexist. Their nationalism anticipated Theodore Roosevelt's progressive "new nationalism." Republican nationalism, in its concern with the advancement of humanity, outlined future trends. Despite partisan rhetoric, Republican speeches, with their concern for American unity, contained a touch of idealism.

V *Liberal Challenge*

Confronting the formidable challenge of ousting a Civil War hero from the White House, Liberals and Democrats waged a tougher campaign than their opponents. Their speeches sometimes made better sense because they recognized what Grant Republicans wanted to ignore: the failures of the Civil War and Reconstruction. All Americans recalled the tragedy of civil war, but the Republicans stressed its successful results and drew their lessons from it. Their opponents responded emotionally to the tragedies, and complained that the disharmonies released had not diminished. The rhetoric of such men as Sumner, Schurz, Horatio Seymour, and Pollard outshone their opponents in compassion. Although their advocacy of traditional nationalism was unrealistic, their appeal to the torn feelings of Americans challenged Republican confidence that the nation was enthusiastically united. Here, Greeley was clearly torn between his recognition of the war's contribution to emancipation and its essential tragedy.

Democrats and Liberals continued to admonish that solutions for a war-torn country lay in restoration and reconciliation. They despised a powerful central government. Only many years of tolerance and common experiences could nurture real nationalism. Republicans were mistaken to claim that a new nationalism had arisen from the

Civil War. They misunderstood the meaning of nationalism. A nation's sense of identity lay in its collective and cumulative memory, in its association with its dead, and with those yet to be born. Nationalism could never be created artificially by an institution like government, nor could national feelings be stimulated that way. Democrats and Liberals sought to bypass the Civil War and link nationalism with the values of an enlightened past: individualism, voluntarism, freedom, mobility, regionalism, and equality.

Often opposition arguments on nationalism centered on the character of President Grant. Unlike twentieth-century observers, Americans in 1872 did not view Grant as a weak president. Grant had emerged from the Civil War as an Herculean military chieftain who enforced the Ku Klux Klan Act in the South and promoted his expansionist schemes abroad. Sumner and Schurz portrayed Grant as a potential dictator, a usurper of public power, and consequently a destroyer of traditional nationalism. Grant's wartime habit of crushing the opposition had persisted in peace: he excited the passions of a divided people rather than conciliated them. With his corrupt Reconstruction policies, Grant had purchased conflict at a time when consensus was paramount. He had betrayed his 1868 slogan, "Let us have peace."

Of all Grant's opponents, the three most notable Liberals—Greeley, Sumner, and Schurz—made significant contributions to a definition of American nationalism. Their thought was particularly significant, because all three had undergone transformations in their ideas on nationalism since the 1860s; they partially abandoned the concept of the nation-state in favor of reemphasizing traditional nationalism.

Of these three, Sumner was the unlikeliest Liberal recruit. The fiery champion of blacks and nationalism now found himself associated with former slave owners and fomenters of rebellion. In 1867, he had described a nationalism which incorporated a growing central government. Although ill in 1872 and unable to participate actively in the campaign, he had apparently shifted his thinking. He no longer demanded active federal protection of the black franchise. Instead he asked that federal troops be withdrawn in the interest of harmony. The hope of the nation lay in Greeley who, as an antislavery advocate, had the ability to bring the discordant races together. Sumner admonished that only by sympathetic cooperation could racism end. He wished to "seize the opportunity to make the equal rights of all secure through peace and reconciliation."[10]

Sumner claimed to place peace "above all things except the Rights of Man"; but in truth, by 1872 his vision of peace eclipsed the cause of equality. Sumner's commitment to American nationalism was deep, and he could not imagine a national reconciliation without peace. For this goal, Sumner was ready to sacrifice much. Some critics predicted that once Sumner's beloved peace became reality, as it did in 1877, it would herald the beginnings of a systematic repression of Southern blacks. Sumner never lived to see this, for in 1874 he died. Like the rest of the country, after a long struggle with its conscience, Sumner was tired and wanted only calm. The quest for equality was over; the old vitality was gone.[11]

Like Sumner, Schurz, the Liberal Republican senator from Missouri and the titular leader of Liberal Republicans, emphasized themes of national peace and reconciliation. Despite his initial opposition to Greeley's nomination, Schurz campaigned diligently for the ticket until November, and no man articulated the goals of Liberals more eloquently. His emphasis of the Liberal movement as a champion of popular nationalism reflected most Liberals' concern with the meaning and fate of this American phenomenon.[12]

In his keynote address and in later speeches, Schurz stressed the national character of the Liberal movement. When Liberals bolted from the Republican party, they abandoned partisanship and embraced freedom, equality, and peace. These ideals were currently threatened by the corruption, apathy, and partisanship which had characterized the Reconstruction era and the Grant administration. The Civil War and Reconstruction had strained the energies of the people.

Schurz believed that the rebirth of American national feeling depended on the federal government's policy toward the South. Like other Liberals and Democrats, Schurz defined the nation as a unit inspiring fraternal sentiment. The South had in fact been secessionist minded in 1865 and 1866, but he was convinced that by 1872 the South wanted to return to the nation. The best way to achieve this was to restore her commitment to the American nation, not to force her physically into compliance. It was essential to reanimate "a fraternal and friendly National feeling," to revive the national "impulses" in Southern hearts, to restore a "hearty reconciliation," to pursue a policy of renationalization which "binds together the hearts of the people and not their bodies only." The government must appear as a friend, not as an oppressor of the South.[13]

Like most northern Republicans, Schurz evoked a new nation, a "new order of things," based on a higher plane of morality. But Schurz's sense of novelty often belied a genuine desire to revert to a purer and more innocent American past. He spoke about renationalizing, about reuniting, about reanimating basic sentiments.

His reconciliation theme was as much a compromise of time sequences between past and present, as a reconciliation among people. As an immigrant, Schurz had come to America "to enjoy the blessings of republican government and to live in the moral pride of a free man. I cannot sacrifice both." Schurz could not forget his early dreams of youth; his dilemma was that the gap between past dreams and present reality could not be bridged.[14]

VI Greeley's Campaign

Greeley developed similar themes of reconciliation. His vast experience underlined one fact: his career was representative of what America had endured in his lifetime. He had articulated the contradictory American appeals of city and frontier, of peace and war, of politics and privacy, of reform and conservatism, of revolution and order, that had blazed throughout the nineteenth century. As Glyndon Van Deusen has shown, Greeley had for many years espoused a theory of national unity, based on economic integration and popular consent. His nomination was the epitome of his long career and intense ambition., but he also saw himself as the man of unity, a savior, who might restore light to America after its nightmare of war and reconstruction. At one campaign stop, he said that the South was a "lost cause, but . . . not a lost people. . . . They have come back to us under compulsion . . . but I wish to change that compulsion into affection, for that is statesmanship. That work I am seeking, as far as I can, to do."[15]

In pursuit of his mission to reunite the nation, Greeley, in the last two weeks of September, conducted a vigorous speaking tour across half the nation. In New Jersey, Pennsylvania, Ohio, Kentucky, and Indiana, Greeley delivered a series of speeches which were remarkable because, while elaborating the same themes, each was distinctly different, each developing his concept of American nationalism.

During his campaign, Greeley stressed the theme of communication among Americans, as he had in other writings. Part of the secret of a reborn American nationalism lay in the First Amendment: the exercise of free speech and free press in peaceable assembly. By free discussion, Americans would arouse their hitherto dormant affections for each other. By encouraging "distrust, suspicion and alienation," Grant's administration separated "the hearts of the American people from each other." Greeley asked Americans to "resolve to agree to differ, and be ready to listen to what another has to say, and not be despondent and denounce and prescribe him, because his conviction is not our own." He exhorted Americans to be activists in speaking out—it was better to be activist in argument than in war.[16]

The dilemma of the Civil War haunted Greeley's prose. If an essential unity existed among Americans, why had they fought? Greeley attempted to explain this by suggesting that the war had at least settled the question of secession and of slavery. The Civil War was the American War; each section had fought to preserve what it felt constituted the essence of America. "I believe," said Greeley, "that war of the Union was righteously fought in the interest of no section, of no party, but in the interest of universal humanity." Victory for the Union was not a victory for Republicans or Northerners, but for America. Grant's mistake lay in transforming a national victory into a partisan triumph. Greeley somewhat naively believed that Southerners welcomed Union victory because it emancipated them from the mistakes of the Confederacy and allowed them once again to join American destiny.

Yet he counseled Northerners not to regard their military victory as a vindication of Northern prejudices. It reflected neither sectionalism, nor class, but a victory for all Americans. "Our triumph is the uplifting of every one to the common platform of American liberty and American nationality."[17] Greeley was presenting the concept of a radically benevolent nationalism—not good because it represented great power, but because it symbolized a deeper awareness of men's ultimate bond with other men. Nationalism was enriching because it rose above prejudice, above any taint of racism, sectionalism, or class.

Greeley believed that, despite the tragic consequences of the Civil War, unity would prevail. He spoke of the war as the "dark days," "days of hatred, and strife, and violence, and disruption." He regretted that "we did tear . . . each other; we did destroy." Like the Democratic candidate Horatio Seymour in 1868, Greeley preached a doctrine of love and forgetfulness: "Let us remember only that we have made peace." Let Americans eradicate ugly passions from their souls and embrace themselves as brothers. He wrapped his message in a garment of mysticism: "One sentiment, one purpose animates the American heart, and that is that the union of the States must and shall be preserved."[18]

Greeley understood the feelings of alienation among Americans. Torn by war, embittered by peace, many people had grown indiffer-

116

ent to the national destiny. Greeley exhorted them to care again. He looked to a new American people—"willing, joyful, cordial, united," and "not pinned together by bayonets." He wanted a "union of hearts and hopes and hands." He saw a "better future . . . of concord and of peace, of mutual reliance and sympathy, which was not known in the old time." Of all the candidates since 1864, Horace Greeley was the one who best conveyed a nationalism of tenderness and compassion.[19]

But few listened. The election returns in November spelled crushing defeat for Greeley, his program, and the Liberal Republican movement. Greeley had apparently appealed to a united and strong national sentiment which was not fully there. Grant won a popular mandate by about 700,000 votes over Greeley and managed to carry all but three border and three Southern states. Many Liberals lived to see their views eventually triumph, but Greeley was not one of them.

The "Old White Hat" now knew only profound sadness. His wife had died on October 30. Added to the tragedy of Greeley's last days was his own tendency of self-accusation. In a letter to Mason Tappan, he said that "I have been so . . . assailed that I hardly know whether I have been running for the Presidency or from the Penitentiary." And in a private note, he said bitterly, "I stand naked before God the most utterly, hopelessly wretched and undone of all who ever lived. I have done more harm and wrong than any man who ever saw the light of day." Greeley blamed himself for succumbing to the lure of power. "My fatal vice has been a readiness to believe and trust ever flattering, plausible acclaim. . . . I had been tempted by the glittering bait of the Presidency, but had oftener repelled than courted it. . . . I became a monster-spirit of the cabal against [Grant]."[20]

His postelectoral return to the *Tribune* stimulated a revolt against his editorship. His health diminished, and his mind gave way. On November 29, he died. The nation which he could not reconcile in life momentarily united to mourn his death. His funeral brought both President Grant and Senator Schurz together in New York City to commemorate a great editor. The *Tribune* delivered a glowing eulogy: "We leave his praises to the poor whom he succored, to the lowly whom he lifted up, to the slave whose back he saved from the lash, to the oppressed whose wrongs he made his own."[21]

After twelve years of strife, many Americans were tired and disillusioned. They only wanted peace. But in rejecting Greeley for Grant, a substantial majority registered their belief that physical force was still necessary to achieve that harmony. Conciliation would not work, because the elixir of a united and vital national sentiment was not there. Indeed, a conversation between former President Ulysses Grant and Germany's Otto von Bismarck revealed Grant's own conviction on the need for firm measures. As Edmund Wilson commented, Grant

had become one of the staunchest supporters of the Unionist policy of force, the most illustrious living representative of the powerful political organism which the United States had become. He and Bismarck had much in common, and their agreements were fraternal and emphatic. Each had played a critical role in the unification of his country, and both felt the necessity of maintaining that unity by the exercise of a strong hand.[22]

The meaning of nationalism had become divided between the categories of force and idealism. As a force in foreign affairs, the United States was triumphant. As the ideal of a better and newer world, America seemed a failure, despite the Reconstruction leaders' courageous attempts to integrate blacks into the American system. America's domestic disorders and newly discovered governmental militancy made the country seem very much a replica of an imperial France or a Bismarckian Germany. What Carlton Hayes has said about European nationalism in these years could be applied to what many Americans feared was taking place in America: nationalism was "divested of romantic trappings of altruism and cosmopolitanism," and became self-centered and realistic.

No longer modest or pacific, it grew blatant and bellicose; and with pride of success substituted for mere aspiration, it took on an imperialistic complexion. For a nation which by force of arms had demonstrated its fitness to survive must be superior to others, and entitled, in so far as it could, to dominate them. This type of nationalism was obviously not liberal.[23]

To many Americans blood and iron would rule where the untold possibilities of freedom as articulated by men like Greeley had promised so much. But many Americans, especially Grant Republicans, would not agree with such a gloomy prognosis. They would point to black American progress under government protection. In his *Personal Memoirs*, written some years later, Ulysses Grant continued to emphasize that the Civil War, despite its tragedy, "begot a spirit of independence and enterprise." The country had spread out; it was knit together by railroads; and it was known to all through maps of all its regions. This came from the war, in Grant's view.[24]

But much of the rehetoric, both Republican and Liberal-Democratic, had a desperate tone when it dealt with the disunity of America. Despite the realism of Grant nationalism, nationalism as a spiritual resource seemed dead. A dark mood was abroad in the land. All this was ominous for a nation about to celebrate its centennial year. But Greeley's vision would outlive his times.

CHAPTER 10

Advocate of Democracy

SOME months after Horace Greeley's death, Junius Henri Browne, who had been a crack war correspondent for the *New York Tribune* during the Civil War, wrote a charming tribute for *Harper's New Monthly*. Browne, who had been imprisoned by the Confederates, recalled some of the famous characteristics of his former employer. Browne presented a thoughtful, balanced treatment of the great editor; while recognizing Greeley's defects, he also displayed his generation's appreciation of Greeley's contributions. He underlined basic Greeley qualities which would prove timeless: his American nationalism, his belief in progress, his stimulating intellectuality, his reform zeal.

In his retrospective, Browne made a distinction between superficial, infamous details about Greeley's bearing and the greatness of his being. Browne affectionately cataloged Greeley's annoying habits: his sloppy dress, his "intemperate" invective against others, his childish lack of discipline, his moodiness, his contradictory impulses which moved between conservative and radical perspectives. But Browne claimed that there were many misunderstandings about Greeley: unlike the caricatures, Greeley was concerned with cleanliness in appearance even if "slovenly" in fashion; he was dedicated to improving his "intellect"; he showed unusual physical courage under mob attack in 1863; and most importantly, Greeley was deeply committed to the spirit of American democracy both in principle and in practice. [1]

"A more thorough American, a more genuine democrat, than Horace Greeley never drew breath," said Browne. "Freedom, Progress, Education were the trinity of his moral creed. . . . His constant . . . thought was for the People. . . He was beyond . . . all his predecessors and contemporaries the great democrat of his time, the true Tribune of the People. Rank and station really had no weight with him." Browne particularly appreciated the easy accessibility to Greeley: "He wished to be accessible to everybody, even at the expense of being bored, annoyed, and seriously interrupted in his work. . . . The greatest journalist of his age, the best-known man in the republic, was accessible at all times to the humblest and lowliest of the land."[2]

As Browne said, the "time has not yet come to analyze his complicated and eccentric character, to give him fair and just presentation to the world." But Browne, like many of his contemporaries, remained convinced that Greeley's life had profound implications for American culture: "his struggling life, his heroic battle with hostile circumstance, his courageous climbing from the lowest rung of Fortune's ladder, the inner tragedy of his . . . proud and silent spirit, and his dramatic death, must form one of the most vivid . . . chapters of American history."[3]

Greeley's contributions to the American heritage rest in two areas: the impact of his ideas and activities on his country in his lifetime, and the gift of his many published writings to future generations. Greeley was a vital force in reform movements, especially with the slavery issue, in urban development, in agricultural education, in American journalism, in political affairs, in literary criticism. While he was never a systematic thinker and while he did not develop a consistent philosophy, his adherence to certain American principles of open dialogue, of free press, of democracy, of developing an American national culture, of individualism, of legal rights, made his commentary on the tumultuous events of his time always fascinating, always instructive. And his effective writing style would commend his lasting literary efforts to his descendants. Rarely could responsible adults of his day make a sensible observation without asking, "what did Greeley say?" and rarely can one today ask about the significance of American experience without also asking, "what did Greeley think?"

Three significant Americans could best sum up Greeley's position for posterity. As they reflected on his death some years later, the secretary of state, James G. Blaine, a Republican operative, John Forney, and the Iowa minister, Josiah Grinnell, penned distinctive tributes. Said Blaine,

The controversies which had so recently divided the country were hushed in the presence of death; and all the people, remembering only his noble impulses, his great work for humanity, his broad impress upon the age, united in honoring and mourning one of the most remarkable men in American history.[4]

Said Forney,

What a genius was Horace Greeley! . . . His skill in tracing corrupt motives through all their concealed anatomy; his specific and technical knowledge of great questions; the splendor of his written eloquence; his ready wit; his full, impartial, and accurate insight into the intricate machinery of elections; his simple life; his honesty and truth—all returned to me as, among a thousand others, I saw what was left of all these treasures passing before me on its way to the grave.[5]

Said Grinnell,

Horace Greeley was the unquestioned great journalist of the century. . . . In his latter days his form was bent, and with a wabbling gait, flowing flaxen locks, old white coat, banged hat neck-tie awry, he was a distant remove from that semblance of a tailor-made man—Carlyle's clothes dummy; but the touch of that soft, delicate hand and the parian-white, comely, massive head, the very impersonation of beauty and power, was never jeered save by shallow sacrilegious scribblers, too obtuse to see set on that brow "the seal of a god."[6]

By 1980, after the ravages of Vietnam and Watergate, when the balance between national ideals and power seemed lost, Americans began to realize anew that the riches of the past were indeed open to new discoveries. And there was not a better place to begin than in the writings of Horace Greeley. In his best passages, Greeley bursts to life and reminds us of the glories of things past. Greeley taught his countrymen that theirs was never a land of innocence, never an Eden, that indeed the task before them was continually to recapture the best talents of the people and to forge a society commensurate with their greatest vision, a New World of fresh starts, of independent minds, of equal status. In his writings, there is Greeley exhorting Americans once again to hope, to possibility, to the lure of something better. He had seen the ravages of slavery, and yet also he had witnessed its demise. He had understood the suppression of labor, and yet he foresaw gradual incorporation of the worker into the economic structure. To Greeley, there was failure but never loss; he had confronted corruption of power and won. Americans could open their Greeley and find a renewed commitment to democratic culture in an era of transition from the garden to the machine.[7]

For all his limitations, Greeley had entered the American imagination; for all his practicality, he remained a man of vision. To rediscover Greeley is to rediscover the essence of American existence.

Notes and References

Chapter One

1. Horace Greeley, *The Recollections of a Busy Life* (New York, 1868), pp. 165–66.
2. Whitelaw Reid, *Horace Greeley* (New York, 1879), pp. 20–21.
3. "Our Fourth of July Oration," *New York Tribune*, July 4, 1851 (editorial).
4. John Greenleaf Whittier, letter to Edwin H. Chapin, February 3, 1872, in *Letters of John Greenleaf Whittier*, 3 vols., ed. John W. Pickens (Cambridge, 1978), 3:282.
5. James Parton, *Life of Horace Greeley* (New York, 1855), p. 412.
6. Parton, *Greeley* (Boston, 1882), p. 377.
7. John G. Shortall, "Horace Greeley," in Horace Greeley Papers, Library of Congress, Washington, D.C.
8. Horace Greeley, letter to Moses Cortland, April 14, 1845, Horace Greeley Papers.
9. Horace Greeley, *Glances at Europe* (New York, 1851), pp. 147, 349.
10. A. K. McClure, "Horace Greeley as I Knew Him," *Success*, February 1901, p. 620.
11. Ralph Waldo Emerson, *Journals*, 10 vols. (Boston, 1904–1914), 8:229.
12. J. G. Forman, letter to *New York Tribune*, June 20, 1873, Horace Greeley Papers.
13. Josiah Bushnell Grinnell, *Men and Events of Forty Years* (Boston, 1891), p. 86.
14. Horace Greeley, *Congressional Globe*, February 27, 1849, p. 605.

Chapter Two

1. Greeley, *The Recollections of a Busy Life*, p. 417.
2. Horace Greeley, "Education," *Jeffersonian*, November 10, 1838 (editorial); Horace Greeley, "The Suffrage Question," *New York Tribune*, June 2, 1846.
3. Horace Greeley, "Ode for the Meetings of the Friends of Ireland," in "A Poem by Horace Greeley," by Joel Benton, *Penny Magazine* 1 (1896):11; editorial, *Philadelphia Inquirer*, November 30, 1872.
4. Greeley, "Education," *Jeffersonian*, November 10, 1838 (editorial); Horace Greeley, introduction to *The Writings of Cassius Marcellus Clay*, ed. Horace Greeley (New York, 1848), p. v.

5. James Parton, *Life of Horace Greeley* (Boston, 1882), pp. 104–5.

6. Horace Greeley, "The Fourth of July," *New York Tribune*, July 4, 1846 (editorial).

7. Ibid.

8. Horace Greeley, letter to O. A. Bowen, April 12, 1843, Horace Greeley Papers.

9. Horace Greeley, "Our Country," *New Yorker*, October 15, 1836 (editorial).

10. Horace Greeley, "Commissioner Loring and the Fugitive Slave Act," *New York Tribune*, June 6, 1854 (editorial); Horace Greeley, "Nebraska and Our Duty," *New York Tribune*, May 24, 1854 (editorial); Horace Greeley, *New York Tribune*, May 10, 1854 (editorial).

11. Horace Greeley, "The African Slave Trade," *New York Tribune*, July 3, 1854 (editorial).

12. Horace Greeley, "George Washington's Birthday," *New York Tribune*, February 22, 1864 (editorial).

13. Horace Greeley, "Going to Go" *New York Tribune*, November 9, 1860 (editorial).

14. Horace Greeley, "The Southern Grievance," *New York Tribune*, November 28, 1860 (editorial).

15. Horace Greeley, "Letter to John J. Crittenden," *New York Tribune*, January 7, 1861 (editorial).

16. Horace Greeley, "The Prayer of Twenty Millions," *New York Tribune*, August 20, 1862 (editorial); for a fuller discussion of Lincoln's perspective, see chapter 6.

17. Horace Greeley, "Letter to Abraham Lincoln," *New York Tribune*, August 24, 1862 (editorial).

18. Horace Greeley, "The New Base of Freedom," *New York Tribune*, January 1, 1862 (editorial).

19. Ibid.

20. Ibid.

21. Ibid.

22. Ibid.

23. Ibid.

24. Horace Greeley, "The Last Phase of Reconstruction," *New York Tribune*, January 14, 1867 (editorial); Horace Greeley, "The True Basis of Reconstruction," *New York Tribune*, November 27, 1866 (editorial).

25. Horace Greeley, "Independence Day," *New York Tribune*, July 4, 1862 (editorial); Horace Greeley, "The Day," *New York Tribune*, July 4, 1863 (editorial).

Chapter Three

1. Greeley, "Literature as a Vocation," in *The Recollections of a Busy Life*, pp. 445, 458.

2. Henry David Thoreau, letter to Sophia, July 21, 1843, in F. B. Sanborn, *Henry D. Thoreau* (Boston, 1882), p. 216; Henry David Thoreau, *The Writings of Henry David Thoreau*, ed. Bradford Torrey (Boston, 1906), 7:76. See also Walter Harding, *The Days of Henry Thoreau* (New York, 1965).

3. Horace Greeley, "Lesson for Young Poets." *New York Tribune*, May 25, 1848. See also, Harding, *Days*, p. 213.

4. Greeley, "Lesson for Young Poets," *New York Tribune*, May 25, 1848.

5. Horace Greeley, letter to Henry David Thoreau, August 16, 1846, in Sanborn, *Thoreau*, p. 219.

6. Margaret Fuller, review of the *Narrative of Frederick Douglass*, *New York Tribune*, June 10, 1845. See also Arthur W. Brown, *Margaret Fuller* (New York, 1964); William Harlan Hale, *Horace Greeley: Voice of the People* (New York, 1950); Paula Blanchard, *Margaret Fuller: From Transcendentalism to Revolution* (New York, 1978); the discussion of Margaret Fuller in chapter 7.

7. Greeley, *Recollections*, pp. 171, 175, 179.

8. Margaret Fuller, Letter to Eugene Fuller, February, 1845, in *The Writings of Margaret Fuller*, ed. Mason Wade (New York, 1941), p. 575.

9. Greeley, *Recollections*, p. 180.

10. See Hale, *Greeley* and Glyndon Van Deusen, *Horace Greeley: Nineteenth Century Crusader* (New York, 1953).

11. See Van Deusen, *Greeley*, and Alice Felt Tyler, *Freedom's Ferment: Phases of American Social History: From the Colonial Period to the Outbreak of the Civil War* (Minneapolis, 1944).

Chapter Four

1. Horace Greeley, Letter to William M. Chase et al., May 9, 1856, Horace Greeley Papers; James Parton, *Life of Horace Greeley* (Boston, 1882), pp. 296–97.

2. Horace Greeley, "Emancipation of Labor," in *Hints Toward Reform* (New York, 1850), p. 33.

3. Horace Greeley, "Slavery at Home," in *Hints*, p. 353.

4. Horace Greeley, letter to W. E. Robinson, June 10, 1850, Horace Greeley Papers.

5. Horace Greeley, letter to Beman Brockway, November 19, 1847, and letter to Mrs. Pauline W. Davis, September 1, 1852, Horace Greeley Papers.

6. Greeley, "Emancipation of Labor," in *Hints*, p. 37.

7. Greeley, "Organization of Labor," in *Hints*, pp. 183–84.

8. Ibid., pp. 184–85.

9. Horace Greeley, "Life—The Ideal and the Actual," in *Hints*, pp. 77, 82.

10. Horace Greeley, "Reforms and Reformers," in *The Recollections of a Busy Life*, p. 498.

11. Horace Greeley, "Humanity," in *Hints*, p. 396; Greeley, "Life," in ibid., p. 55.

12. Horace Greeley, "The Social Architects-Fourier," in ibid., p. 292.

Chapter Five

1. Horace Greeley, *An Overland Journey* (1859; reprint ed., New York, 1969), p. xli; see the excellent introduction by Charles Duncan.

2. A.K. McClure, "Horace Greeley as I Knew Him," *Success*, February 1901, p. 620.

3. Greeley, *Overland Journey*, p. 73.

4. Ibid., pp. 132–33.

5. Ibid., p. 119.

6. Ibid., pp. 179–80, 184.

7. Ibid., p. 194.

8. Ibid., pp. 193–94.

9. Ibid., p. 193.

10. Horace Greeley, *Congressional Globe*, February 20, 1849, pp. 608–10.

11. Greeley, *Overland Journey*, p. 185.

12. Ibid., p. 191.

13. Ibid., p. 309.

14. Ibid., p. 326.

Chapter Six

1. Horace Greeley, *Recollections of a Busy Life*, pp. 420–21.

2. David Donald and James G. Randall, *The Civil War and Reconstruction*, 2d ed. (Lexington, 1969), p. 778.

3. Greeley, *Recollections*, p. 424.

4. Ibid.; Horace Greeley, *The American Conflict*, 2 vols. (Hartford, 1864–1867), 1:8.

5. Greeley, *American Conflict*, 1:9, 2:8; Horace Greeley, letter to Salmon P. Chase, December 27, 1863, Salmon P. Chase Papers, Historical Society of Pennsylvania, Philadelphia, Pa.; Greeley, *Recollections*, p. 424.

6. Horace Greeley, letter to Salmon P. Chase, August 16, 1864, Horace Greeley Papers. Greeley, *Recollections*, p. 424.

7. Horace Greeley, letter to Mrs. R. M. Whipple, April 13, 1865, Horace Greeley Papers.

8. Horace Greeley, "The American Experiment," *New York Tribune*, November 27, 1860 (editorial).

9. Greeley, *American Conflict*, 1:18–19.

10. Ibid., 1:33–35.

11. Ibid., 1:40.

12. Ibid., 1:28–30.

13. Ibid., 1:67.

14. Ibid., 1:51.

15. Ibid., 1:67, 70–71.

16. Ibid., 1:82, 142.

17. Ibid., 1:178.

18. Ibid., 1:179, 209, 357.

19. Ibid., 2:255.

20. Ibid., 2:245, 255, 527–28.

21. Ibid., 2:528.

22. Ibid., 2:504, 511.

23. Josiah Grinnell, *Men and Events of Forty Years* (Boston, 1891), pp. 220–21.

24. Greeley, *American Conflict*, 2:562–63.

25. Greeley, letter to Chase, December 27, 1863.

26. Horace Greeley, "The Fruits of the War," *Galaxy* 4 (1867): 364.

27. Ibid., p. 367.

28. Ibid., p. 366.

29. Gideon Welles, *Diary of Gideon Welles*, 3 vols. (New York, 1960), 2:111–12.

30. Abraham Lincoln, "To Horace Greeley," August 22, 1862, in *Collected Works*, ed. Ray Basler (New Brunswick, 1953), 5:388–89; for a full discussion of Greeley's editorial, see chapter 2.

31. Horace Greeley, "An Estimate of Abraham Lincoln," in *Greeley on Lincoln*, ed. Joel Benton (New York, 1893), pp. 23, 74–76; Greeley, *Recollections*, pp. 404, 407.

32. Greeley, "Estimate," p. 63; Greeley, *Recollections*, p. 404.

33. Greeley, *Recollections*, p. 409.

34. Ibid., pp. 308–39.

35. Greeley, "Estimate," pp. 78–79.

Chapter Seven

1. Horace Greeley, *Recollections of a Busy Life*, p. vii.

2. James Parton, *The Life of Horace Greeley* (1855), p. 440.

3. Horace Greeley, "Self-Made Men," as quoted in Dixon Wector, *The Hero in America* (Ann Arbor, 1963), p. 76.

4. Greeley, *Recollections*, p. 429.

5. Ibid., pp. 29, 78.

6. Ibid., pp. 64, 76.

7. Ibid., pp. 20–23.

8. Ibid., p. 28.

9. Ibid., pp. 71, 169.

10. Ibid., pp. 71–73.

11. Ibid., pp. 55–56.

12. Ibid., p. 59.

13. Ibid., p. 60

14. Parton, *The Life of Horace Greeley* (1882), p. 22.

15. Greeley, *Recollections,* p. 417.

16. Ibid., p. 142.

17. Ibid., p. 84.

18. Ibid., pp. 141, 192.

19. Ibid., pp. 145, 147, 192–93.

20. Ibid., p. 148.

21. Ibid., p. 168.

22. Ibid., pp. 175, 179, 191; Horace Greeley, introduction to *Woman in the Nineteenth Century* by Margaret Fuller (New York, 1855), p. ix.

23. Greeley, *Recollections,* p. 143.

24. Ibid., p. 147.

Chapter Eight

1. Horace Greeley, *Essays Designed to Elucidate the Science of Political Economy* (Philadelphia, 1869), p. ix.

2. Ibid., p. 344.

3. Ibid., p. 346.

4. Ibid., p. 51.

5. Horace Greeley, *Recollections of a Busy Life,* p. 295.

6. Horace Greeley, *What I Know of Farming* (New York, 1871), pp. 44–45.

7. Greeley, *Recollections,* pp. 120, 299.

8. Greeley, *What I Know of Farming,* p. 184.

9. Ibid., p. 25.

10. Ibid., pp. 250–51.

11. Ibid., pp. 13–14.

12. Ibid., p. 248.

13. Ibid., p. 255.

Chapter Nine

1. John R. Commons, "Horace Greeley and the Working Class Origins of the Republican Party," *Political Science Quarterly* 24 (1909): 474.

2. Richard Yates, speech at St. Louis, Missouri, November 1, 1872, copied from *St. Louis Democrat,* November 2, 1872 (Jacksonville, Illinois, 1872), pp. 16–17; George F. Hoar, speech at Worcester, Massachusetts, August 13, 1872 (Worcester, 1872), p. 1.

3. Horace Greeley, "Letter of Acceptance" May 20, 1872, in *The Life and Public Career of Hon. Horace Greeley, Liberal Republican Candidate for President* (New York, 1872), p. 71.

4. Kirk H. Porter and Donald Bruce Johnson, *National Party Platforms, 1840–1964* (Urbana, Ill., 1964), p. 44.

5. Henry Adams, *The Education of Henry Adams* (1918; reprint ed., New York, 1931), pp. 264, 266; for background on the Liberal Republicans, see Patrick W. Riddleberger, "The Break in the Radical Ranks: Liberals vs. Stalwarts in the Election of 1872," *Journal of Negro History* 44 (April 1959):136–57; Earle Dudley Ross, *The Liberal Republican Movement* (New York, 1919); for background on the campaign, see William Gillette, "Election of 1872," Arthur M. Schlesinger, Jr., and Fred L. Israel, eds., *History of American Presidential Elections, 1789–1968*, 4 vols. (New York, 1971); William B. Hesseltine, *Ulysses S. Grant, Politician* (New York, 1935); James Ford Rhodes, *History of the United States*, 8 vols. (New York, 1902–1920); Eugene Roseboom, *History of Presidential Elections* (New York, 1964).

6. Eric McKitrick, *Andrew Johnson and Reconstruction* (Chicago, 1960), pp. 341–42.

7. Carl Schurz, "The Aims of the Liberal Republican Movement" [speech at Cincinnati, Ohio, May 2, 1872], in *Speeches, Correspondence and Political Papers of Carl Schurz*, ed. Frederick Bancroft, 6 vols. (New York, 1913), 2:356.

8. Edward A. Pollard, *A Southern Historian's Appeal for Horace Greeley* (Lynchburg, 1872), p. 16.

9. Porter and Johnson, *National Party Platforms*, pp. 46–48. For more on Grant's Southern policy see Roger D. Bridges, "President Grant and the Formation of a Southern Policy, 1869–1877," paper delivered at U.S. Grant Symposium, Wright State University (Fairborn, Ohio), May 6, 1972.

10. Charles Sumner, "Republicanism vs. Grantism: The Presidency a Trust, Not a Plaything and a Perquisite; Personal Government and Presidential Pre-Tensions; Reform and Purity in Government," speech in the Senate, May 31, 1872; "Greeley or Grant?" speech intended for delivery at Boston, Massachusetts, September 3, 1872; "Interest and Duty of Colored Citizens in the Presidential Election," letter to Colored Citizens, July 29, 1872; Charles Sumner, letter to James G. Blaine, August 5, 1872, in *The Works of Charles Sumner*, ed. Francis V. Balch, 15 vols. (Boston, 1873–1883), 15:85–157, 191–94, 197, 213, 228–29, 241, 254.

11. Sumner, "Interest . . . of Colored Citizens," p. 192.

12. Carl Schurz, letter to Horace Greeley, May 6, 1872, in *Papers*, 2:361–68.

13. Schurz, "Aims of the Liberal Republican Movement," p. 356; Schurz, "Why Anti-Grant," in *Papers*, pp. 395, 400–401, 413–14.

14. Schurz, "Why Anti-Grant," pp. 393, 426.

15. Horace Greeley, speech at Dayton, Ohio, September 24, 1872, *New York Tribune*, September 25, 1872. See also Glyndon Van Deusen, "The Nationalism of Horace Greeley," ed. Edward M. Earle, *Nationalism and Internationalism: Essays Inscribed to Carlton J. H. Hayes* (New York, 1950), pp. 431–54.

16. Greeley, speech at Pittsburgh, Pa.; Greeley, speech at Danville, Pennsylvania, September 26, 1872, *New York Tribune*, September 27, 1872.

17. Horace Greeley, speech at Cincinnati, Ohio, September 20, 1872, *New York Tribune*, September 21, 1872; Horace Greeley, speech at Newark, Ohio, September 20, 1872, ibid., September 21, 1872; Horace Greeley, speech at Hamilton, Ohio, 24 September 1872, ibid., September 25, 1872.

18. Horace Greeley, speech at Newport, Kentucky, September 22, 1872, ibid., September 23, 1872; Greeley, speech at Hamilton; Greeley, speech at Cincinnati.

19. Horace Greeley, speech at Jeffersonville, Indiana, September 23, 1872, ibid., September 24, 1872; Greeley, speech at Hamilton; Greeley, speech at Dayton; Greeley, speech at Newport.

20. Horace Greeley, letter to Mason Tappan, November 8, 1872, Horace Greeley Papers, Horace Greeley, private memo, November 13, 1872, Horace Greeley Papers, New York Public Library.

21. For information on Greeley's funeral, see *New York Tribune, A Memorial for Horace Greeley* (New York, 1873), and *New York Tribune*, November 30–December 5, 1872.

22. Edmund Wilson, *Patriotic Gore: Studies in the Literature of the American Civil War* (New York, 1962), pp. 169–70.

23. Carlton J. H. Hayes, *A Generation of Materialism, 1871–1900* (New York, 1941), p. 243.

24. Ulysses S. Grant, *Personal Memoirs of U. S. Grant* (New York, 1880–1886), 2:552–53.

Chapter Ten

1. Junius Henri Browne, "Horace Greeley," *Harper's New Monthly Magazine* 46 (1873):735, 737.

2. Ibid., p. 739.

3. Ibid., p. 741.

4. James G. Blaine, *Twenty Years of Congress*, 2 vols. (Norwich, 1886), 2:536.

5. John W. Forney, *Anecdotes of Public Men*, 2 vols. (New York, 1874–1881), 2:212.

6. Josiah Bushnell Grinnell, *Men and Events of Forty Years* (Boston, 1891), p. 220.

7. See Leo Marx, *The Machine in the Garden: Technology and the Pastoral Ideal in America* (New York, 1964).

Selected Bibliography

There are numerous lists of Greeleyania. See the bibliographies in the Van Deusen and Hale biographies for a beginning. The following is highly selective; see "Notes and References" for other sources. Reminiscences of various associates of Greeley like Dana, Schurz, and Weed are helpful. There are other important papers than those cited here.

PRIMARY SOURCES

1. Manuscripts
Papers at the Library of Congress; Chappaqua Historical Society; New York Public Library includes Greeley/Schuyler Colfax letters; and in the Salmon P. Chase Papers at Historical Society of Pennsylvania.

2. Published Works
The American Conflict. 2 vols. Hartford: O. D. Case & Company, 1864, 1866.
The American Laborer. New York: Greeley & McElrath, 1843.
Art and Industry. New York: Redfield, 1853.
Association Discussed. New York: 1847.
Editorials. *The Jeffersonian, The Log Cabin, New-Yorker, New York Tribune.*
Essays Designed to Elucidate the Science of Political Economy. Philadelphia: Porter & Coates, 1869.
Glances at Europe. New York: DeWitt & Davenport, 1851.
Hints Toward Reforms. New York: Harper & Brothers, 1850.
A History of the Struggle for Slavery Extension or Restriction in the United States. New York: Dix, Edwards & Co., 1856.
Mr. Greeley's Letters from Texas. New York: Tribune Office, 1871.
An Overland Journey from New York to San Francisco, in the summer of 1859. Reprint, New York: Alfred A. Knopf, 1969.
Recollections of a Busy Life. New York: J. B. Ford & Co., 1868.
What I Know of Farming, New York: C. W. Carleton & Co., 1971.

SECONDARY SOURCES

1. Books
BAEHR, HARRY W., JR. *The New York Tribune Since the Civil War.* New York: Dodd, Mead & Co., 1936
BENTON, JOEL, ed. *Greeley on Lincoln.* New York: Baker and Taylor Co., 1893.
BLAINE, JAMES G. *Twenty Years of Congress.* 2 vols. Norwich: Henry Bill, 1886.

CORNELL, WILLIAM. *Life and Public Career of the Hon. Horace Greeley.* Boston: Lee & Shepherd, 1872.

DONALD, DAVID. *Charles Sumner and the Coming of the Civil War.* New York: Charles Scribner's, 1960.

———. *Charles Sumner and the Rights of Man.* New York: Alfred A. Knopf, 1970. The Donald volumes comprise a superior biography of a man, who, like Greeley, was caught in a tension between principle and power.

FORNEY, JOHN W. *Anecdotes of Public Men,* New York: Harper & Brothers, 1874–1881.

GRINNELL, JOSIAH BUSHNELL. *Men and Events of Forty Years.* Boston: D. Lothrop Co., 1891. Filled with charming anecdotes by the man who was the recipient of the advice, "Go West, young man."

HALE, WILLIAM HARLAN. *Horace Greeley: Voice of the People.* Harper, 1950. A delightful, solid biography. One of the best of the recent treatments.

HORNER, HARLAN HOYT. *Lincoln and Greeley.* Champagne: University of Illinois Press, 1953. Solid, but not fully comprehensive.

HUNTINGTON, DAVID CAREN. *Art and the Excited Spirit: America in the Romantic Period.* Ann Arbor: University of Michigan Art Museum, 1972. An original, unique interpretation.

INGERSOLL, L. D. *The Life of Horace Greeley.* Philadelphia: John E. Potter and Co., 1874. Important early biography.

ISELEY, PETER ALLEN. *Horace Greeley, and the Republican Party, 1853–1861.* Princeton: Princeton University Press, 1947. Acclaimed by all as an indispensable source.

LINN, WILLIAM ALEXANDER. *Horace Greeley: Founder and Editor of the New York Tribune.* New York: D. Appleton and Co., 1903. One of Appleton's Series of Historic Lives, this book provides a serviceable narrative account.

MILLER, DOUGLAS T. *Birth of Modern America, 1820–1850.* New York: Pegasus, 1970. A vital interpretation of Greeley's era.

NAGEL, PAUL C. *One Nation Indivisible: The Union in American Thought, 1776–1861.* New York: Oxford University Press, 1964, Comprehensive, excellent.

———. *This Sacred Trust: American Nationality, 1789–1898.* New York: Oxford University Press, 1971. One of the most important books concerning American nationalism; an essential source.

NYE, RUSSEL B. *Society and Culture in America, 1830–1860.* New York: Harper & Row, 1974. A vital study for the national culture of Greeley's formative years.

PARRINGTON, VERNON LOUIS. *Main Currents in American Thought.* 3 vols. New York: Harcourt, Brace & Co. 1927. The second volume, *The Romantic Revolution in America,* contains an excellent chapter, "Horace Greeley: Yankee Radical."

PARTON, JAMES. *The Life of Horace Greeley.* Boston: Houghton, Mifflin Co., 1882. First published in 1855, this book remains one of the most charming, essential studies of Greeley by America's greatest biographer; Parton interviewed Greeley and others.

PERKINS, HOWARD, ed. *Northern Editorials on Secession.* New York: Appleton-Century, 1942.

REAVIS, L. U. *A Representative Life of Horace Greeley.* New York: G. W. Carleton & Co., 1872. Virtually a campaign biography, it contains an important tribute by Cassius M. Clay.

ROURKE, CONSTANCE. *Trumpets of Jubilee.* New York: Harcourt, Brace & Co., 1927. Recognized as a classic, this work gives a brilliant portrait of Greeley as America's spokesman.

SEITZ, DON C. *Horace Greeley: Founder of the New York Tribune.* Indianapolis: Bobbs-Merrill, 1926. A competent treatment; good documentation.

SOTHERAN, CHARLES. *Horace Greeley and Other Pioneers of American Socialism.* New York: Humboldt, 1892.

STODDARD, HENRY LUTHER. *Horace Greeley: Printer, Editor, Crusader.* New York: G. D. Putman's, 1946. Useful study by a man who once saw Greeley as an old man.

STONE, IRVING. *They Also Ran: The Story of the Men Who Were Defeated for the Presidency.* New York: Doubleday & Co., 1943. Begins with a well-written profile of Greeley, based largely on Seitz's biography.

VAN DEUSEN, GLYNDON G. *Horace Greeley: Nineteenth-Century Crusader.* Philadephia: University of Pennsylvania, 1953. The most authoritative recent biography; it presents an appreciative but not uncritical view of Greeley. Essential, well documented.

ZABRISKIE, FRANCIS N. *Horace Greeley, the Editor.* New York: Funk & Wagnalls, 1890. Part of a series, it has a full chapter devoted to Greeley's authorship.

2. Articles

ANDERSON, DAVID H. "Horace Greeley on Michigan's Upper Peninsula." *Inland Seas* 17 (Winter 1961):301–6. Helpful.

BONNER, THOMAS. "Horace Greeley and the Secession Movement." *Mississippi Valley Historical Review* 38 (1952): 425–44. A convincing case for Greeley.

COMMONS, JOHN R. "Horace Greeley and the Working Class Origins of the Republican Party." *Political Science Quarterly* 24 (1909): 469–88.

HALE, WILLIAM HARLAN. "When Karl Marx Worked for Horace Greeley." *American Heritage* 8 (April 1957): 20–25, 110–11. The most thorough treatment available on the unique relationship between the two men who apparently never met.

NEVINS, ALLAN. "Greeley, Horace." In *Dictionary of American Biography.* (1934). The best short introduction available.

ROSS, EARLE D. "Horace Greeley and the South, 1865–1872." *South Atlantic Quarterly* 9 (1916): 324–38.

———. "Horace Greeley and the West." *Mississippi Valley Historical Re-*

view 20 (1933–1934): 63–74. Both the Ross pieces are excellent treatises on Greeley's ideas about expansion.

SHAPIRO, FRED C. "The Life and Death of a Great Newspaper." *American Heritage* 18 (October 1967): 97–112. An excellent short history.

VAN DEUSEN, GLYNDON G. "The Nationalism of Horace Greeley." In *Nationalism and Internationalism: Essays Inscribed to Carlton J. H. Hayes.* New York: Columbia University Press, 1950. pp. 431–54. An excellent treatise.

Index